THE HEIRESS

A Play

by

RUTH and AUGUSTUS GOETZ

Based on the novel
Washington Square
by
HENRY JAMES

SAMUEL FRENCH

LONDON

NEW YORK TORONTO SYDNEY HOLLYWOOD

THE HEIRESS

Produced at the Haymarket Theatre, London, on February 1st, 1949, with the following cast of characters:

(in the order of their appearance)

MARIA (the Parlour-maid)	*Pauline Jameson*
DR AUSTIN SLOPER	*Ralph Richardson*
MRS LAVINIA PENNIMAN (his Sister) . . .	*Gillian Lind*
CATHERINE (his Daughter)	*Peggy Ashcroft*
MRS ELIZABETH ALMOND (his Sister) . . .	*Madge Compton*
MARIAN ALMOND (his Niece)	*Gillian Howell*
ARTHUR TOWNSEND (MARIAN's Fiancé) . . .	*Donald Sinden*
MORRIS TOWNSEND (ARTHUR's Cousin) . . .	*James Donald*
MRS MONTGOMERY (MORRIS's Sister) . . .	*Ann Wilton*

The Play directed by JOHN GIELGUD

SYNOPSIS OF SCENES

The action of the play passes in the front parlour of Dr Sloper's house in Washington Square, in the year 1850

ACT I—SCENE 1   An October evening
      SCENE 2   An afternoon two weeks later
      SCENE 3   The next morning

ACT II—SCENE 1   An April night six months later
      SCENE 2   Two hours later
      SCENE 3   A morning three days later
      SCENE 4   A summer evening almost two years later

THE HEIRESS

ACT I

SCENE I

SCENE.—*The front parlour of* DR SLOPER'S *house in Washington Square. An October evening. 1850.*

The room is a handsome one and has two tall, sash-type windows R. which overlook the Square. Through them can be seen the iron railings of the house, a lamp-post, and one pillar of the portico. The fireplace is in the wall L., which is a convex curve and terminates down L. in a door opening into the study. The back wall contains a large square opening, outlined by pilasters. Two steps, the width of the opening, rise up to the hall and to a pair of sliding doors which can cut it off from the room. Facing the opening and slightly to R. of it, the staircase curves away to L., with a window half-way up. The front door, at the R. end of the hall, is out of sight, and has two steps down into the street. Between the stairs and the front door, another door is partly seen which opens into a clothes closet. Access to the kitchen is below the stairs to L. The house is not decorated in the gaudy Victorian style which we have come to associate with all nineteenth-century interiors. DR SLOPER set up housekeeping with his young bride in 1820 and he and she were in a position in life to buy " Duncan Phyfe's " furniture, and to combine it with the English mahogany which their forbears had brought with them. His tastes have certainly not changed in the years which have elapsed since that time, and so the house which he built for himself is furnished with discretion and elegance. Only in the elaborate drapes and hangings that mask the windows does the new taste for opulence betray itself, and even that is modified. The mantelpiece, the mirror over it, the "Gilbert Stuart" family portraits of MRS SLOPER'S family, these are the indications of the DOCTOR'S affluence. Gilt and red plush would have offended a man of taste as much in 1850 as they would in 1940. A single-headed couch stands R.C., up and down stage, with a small octagonal pedestal table above it. Up R. of the table is a tall upholstered stool. A single chair stands down R., below the windows. In the bay of the downstage window is a strong lacquer coffee-table. Between the windows there is a small writing bureau with a chair to it. In the corner up R. is a large round table, and an oblong table stands in the corner up L. A wing armchair stands in front of the fireplace, with a small cabinet table L. of it. A long, low, fireside stool and a *small circular footstool stand against the fender. Below the fireplace is a pedestal sewing table and a chair with a pole-screen against the wall behind it. A flower-stand with a bowl of flowers on it stands down L. below the door. The windows are fitted with venetian blinds, deep pelmets and long curtains. The floor is parquet with a large circular " Aubusson" carpet and rugs at the door down L. and fireplace. At night the room is lit by oil-lamps, of which there are two on the mantelpiece, one on the writing bureau and a twin pattern on the table up R. There are twin lustre-brackets with candles on the walls R. and L. of the opening up C. A china bell-pull is set in the wall L. of the opening up C. Three small portraits in oils hang on the wall over the writing bureau and there is a large mirror over the mantelpiece. Vases of flowers and ornaments complete the furnishing of the room. The study down L. contains a writing table, with an armchair R. of it and a small chair L. of it. Along the back wall is a leather couch with a filing cabinet L. of it. There is a window in the L. wall with velvet curtains to it. The fireplace backs on to that of the drawing-room and only the fender and mantelpiece are seen. Prints and watercolours hang on the back wall, and the floor is carpeted. At night the study is lit by an oil-lamp that stands on the writing table. Several large medicine jars stand on the filing cabinet. The hall is furnished with an oblong table L. of the foot of the stairs with a narrow oak bench L. of it. Under the table there is a small square stool. A large vase, used for sticks and umbrellas, stands R. of the table, behind the newel post. Another large vase stands in a niche in the staircase wall. Higher up the stairs, three portraits in oils hang on the wall. The staircase is carpeted and both lace and velvet curtains hang at the window. At night the hall is lit by an oil-lamp that stands on the table. A large portrait hangs at the top of the stairs, and another over the door to the clothes closet. (See the Ground Plan at the end of the Play.)*

When the CURTAIN *rises the lamps are lit and a fire burns in the grate.* MARIA, *the parlour-maid, is closing the curtains of the window down* R. *The front door is heard to open, then close.* DR SLOPER *enters the hall from* R. *and moves to the foot of the stairs. He is a distinguished, middle-aged man, impeccably dressed and pleasant in manner. He carries a walking-stick, gloves and medical bag. He puts the walking-stick in the vase, and his hat and gloves on the hall table.*

MARIA (*with a curtsy*). Good evening, Doctor.
SLOPER. Good evening, Maria.
MARIA. Would you like your supper now, Doctor ?

(SLOPER *enters the room and brings his medical bag with him.*)

SLOPER. Have Miss Catherine and her aunt waited for me ?

MARIA. No, sir. They dined quite early. They wanted plenty of time to dress.

SLOPER (*remembering*). Oh yes. (*He glances at the clock.*) Well, our company won't be here for a while.

MARIA (*moving above the table* C.). No, sir. Cook has kept everything warm. Can I bring you a tray?

SLOPER (*putting his bag on the floor* R. *of the armchair*). No, thank you, Maria. (*He sits in the armchair.*) I had a little something at the Garrisons.

MARIA. How is Mrs Garrison?

SLOPER. She is fine—fine. She is the mother of a new citizen. He and I shook hands for the first time at exactly a quarter past six.

MARIA. It's a boy?

SLOPER. Yes.

MARIA. How nice. (*She pours out a glass of sherry.*) They wanted a boy, didn't they?

SLOPER. They just wanted a child, Maria, and now they've got one—eight and a half pounds. Such beautiful little creatures. Why don't they grow up that way?

(MARIA *takes the glass of sherry on the tray to* SLOPER.)

(*Taking the sherry.*) Maria, when you marry, you must have a lot of children. Don't put all your hopes on one. (*He drinks.*)

MARIA (*smiling*). That's what my mother said—she had thirteen. (*She replaces the tray on the table* C.)

SLOPER. Where is my daughter, Maria?

MARIA. Miss Catherine is upstairs, sir.

SLOPER (*rising, putting his glass on the mantelpiece and crossing to the desk*). I must register that birth. Oh, Maria, Mr Garrison will come by at the side door later tonight for a copy of the document. I'll leave it out for you. (*He sits at the desk.*)

MARIA (*picking up the medical bag*). I'll see that he gets it, sir.

(*She exits with the bag down* L. MRS PENNIMAN *enters and comes down the stairs.*)

MRS PENNIMAN (*calling*). Is that you, Austin?

(*She enters the room.*)

SLOPER. Good evening, Lavinia. (*He takes the Certificate Book and the cylinder from the drawer.*)

MRS PENNIMAN. How nice that you are home. I was afraid the baby might take all evening, and then our little party would be spoiled.

SLOPER. No, the baby kept his engagement promptly.

(MARIA *enters down* L. *closing the door behind her.*)

MARIA. Excuse me. What time shall I serve the collation, Doctor?

SLOPER. What time did Miss Catherine suggest ? (*He enters some particulars on the certificate.*)

MARIA. She said to ask you.

SLOPER ⎫
MRS PENNIMAN ⎬ (*together*). ⎰ Well, I should . . .
Serve it . . . (*She looks towards* SLOPER *with an apologetic laugh, then turns to* MARIA.) Serve it late. (*She is embarrassed at her own effrontery.*) Well, I would like a long visit with sister Elizabeth. And I'm anxious to get to know Marian's young man.

SLOPER (*pleasantly*). Serve it late, Maria.

MARIA (*moving up* C.). Yes, sir.

(*She exits up* C. *to* L. MRS PENNIMAN, *anxious to tell* SLOPER *her news, moves below the downstage end of the couch.*)

MRS PENNIMAN. Austin, I had the most exciting time today. (*She sits on the downstage end of the couch.*)

SLOPER (*surprised*). With Catherine ?

MRS PENNIMAN. Oh, no, Catherine was busy. I went out alone. (*She prepares to tell an exciting story.*) Now you might not approve of this, but I strolled into the *Astor Hotel* all by myself.

SLOPER (*amused*). Lavinia ! What a daring thing to do. How did you like the oil paintings over the Bar ?

MRS PENNIMAN. The Bar ? Oh, Austin ! Shame on you ! I didn't go there to drink—I wanted to see the grand staircase. (*She looks across the back of the couch.*) Oh, a birth certificate ! And as I stood there admiring it, I heard a voice behind me saying, " Isn't that Lavinia Penniman ? " I turned around, and who do you suppose it was ?

SLOPER. Could it have been a fellow Poughkeepsiean ?

MRS PENNIMAN. Two of them !

SLOPER. Good gracious, what a windfall ! (*He tears the certificate out and replaces the book in the drawer.*)

MRS PENNIMAN. They had been members of my husband's congregation. And do you know—they have not set foot in that church since he passed away. They said it would be hard to fill the Reverend Penniman's place in the community.

(SLOPER *rises and crosses to* C. *with the certificate and cylinder.*)

SLOPER (*meditatively*). Yes—he was a large man.

MRS PENNIMAN. And then they asked me where I was stopping and when I told them with my brother Dr Sloper at sixteen, Washington Square, they were so impressed. It's just made my visit.

SLOPER (*rolling the certificate*). Then you couldn't have told them what a dreary time we're giving you.

MRS PENNIMAN. Oh, Austin, you're not. I've enjoyed being with you and Catherine.

SLOPER. Have you really, Lavinia? Have you enjoyed it enough to stay on? I have been wondering if you'd care to spend the winter here.

MRS PENNIMAN (*pleased*). Here? Would you like me to?

SLOPER (*putting the certificate in the cylinder*). Yes. I have been asked to represent our doctors at a medical congress in Paris in December.

MRS PENNIMAN (*deeply impressed*). Paris, France?

SLOPER (*smiling*). Yes. (*He resumes his thought.*) Of course, Catherine is of an age where she can perfectly well stay alone with the servants, but I thought if you lived here while I was away, you might help her.

MRS PENNIMAN. Help her? But help her how? She goes out very little, she hardly needs me as a chaperon. She runs this house most competently. She obviously doesn't want a confidante, so what am I to help her to?

SLOPER. Well, for instance, this evening while our company is here. Perhaps you could persuade Catherine to remain quietly in the room with us and join in the conversation.

MRS PENNIMAN. But, Austin, of course she will do that.

SLOPER. The last time I had guests she disappeared into the pantry four successive times.

MRS PENNIMAN. Oh! Well, I will try. And of course I will gladly stay the winter.

SLOPER. Good! Now, my dear, if you will excuse me, I must go and dress. (*He starts to go, but turns back to her.*) Help her to be clever, Lavinia. I should so like her to be a clever woman.

MRS PENNIMAN. But she is so gentle and good.

SLOPER. You are good for nothing unless you are clever.

(*A church clock off is heard to strike the half hour.* SLOPER *goes into the hall, puts the cylinder on the hall table, then exits up the stairs.* MRS PENNIMAN *rises, moves to the fireplace, sits on the firestool and uses the bellows on the fire.* CATHERINE SLOPER *enters, descends the stairs and comes into the room. She is a healthy, quiet girl in her late twenties. She is dressed in an over-elaborate red velvet gown with red trimmings.*)

MRS PENNIMAN (*turning on the firestool*). Catherine. Oh, you've got it on!

CATHERINE. Yes. Do you like the colour?

MRS PENNIMAN. Yes, it's extremely rich.

CATHERINE. Do you think father will like it?

MRS PENNIMAN. He's bound to. You know, one of the last

A*

times I ever saw your poor mother she was wearing the most delicious little bows of that colour in her hair.

CATHERINE. Yes, Aunt, I know. You said they were cherry red.

MRS PENNIMAN. So they were. (*She puts down the bellows.*)

CATHERINE. I picked it up at the dressmaker's on my way to the Hospital Committee this afternoon. The ladies all thought it was a lovely colour. (*She crosses down* L.) Is father in his study ?

MRS PENNIMAN (*rising*). No, he's upstairs dressing. Tell me about the meeting. Did you have a nice time ?

CATHERINE (*crossing to the couch and arranging the cushions*). Some of the women are so foolish that they are funny. They think it ill-bred to know anything about food, so they are useless on the committee. One girl asked me today if veal was the front or the hind part of the cow.

MRS PENNIMAN (*smiling*). What did you tell her ?

CATHERINE (*with humour*). Well, Aunt, I told her the truth. I said it was a nursing calf, and just when it was most adorable, most touching—we *eat* it. (*She sits on the downstage end of the couch.*)

MRS PENNIMAN (*laughing*). Such airs and graces. When I was young we took pride in our housewifery. When I think of the meals I used to set before the Reverend Penniman . . .

CATHERINE (*teasing*). Then you have deceived me, Aunt.

MRS PENNIMAN (*surprised*). How so ?

CATHERINE. You led me to believe that you and he lived on love alone.

(*They laugh.*)

MRS PENNIMAN. Oh, Catherine ! (*She moves to* L. *of her.*) Catherine, dear—er—since you are so handsomely dressed you will allow Maria to attend to all the details of the collation this evening ?

CATHERINE. They are already attended to.

MRS PENNIMAN. Good. (*She sits above* CATHERINE *on the couch.*) Then you won't have any reason to go into the pantry —will you ?

CATHERINE (*after a pause*). You have been talking to father.

MRS PENNIMAN. Well, in a way—I have. You see, dear, your father feels . . .

CATHERINE (*rising and moving* C.). Father would like me to be composed and to direct the conversation.

MRS PENNIMAN. Yes.

CATHERINE. But I can't. That is why I go into the pantry.

MRS PENNIMAN. But, dear, perhaps you do not try sufficiently ?

CATHERINE. Oh, I do, I do. I would do anything to please

him.   There is nothing that means more to me than that.   (*Confidingly.*)   I've sat upstairs sometimes and thought of things I should say, and how I should say them, but when I am in company—I lose it all.

MRS PENNIMAN.   But why, Catherine ?   With me you express yourself on every subject.

CATHERINE.   When I am here in the parlour with father, it seems that no-one could want to listen to *me*.   No matter what I have thought about upstairs, down here it seems so unimportant.

MRS PENNIMAN.   Well, Catherine, dear, if you will observe your cousin Marian this evening, you will see that what she says is never of any great consequence, but that doesn't keep her from saying it.

CATHERINE (*moving down* L.).   Yes, Aunt, but Marian might recite the alphabet, and Arthur Townsend would still think her the cleverest girl in New York.   (*She sits on the chair down* L.)

MRS PENNIMAN.   Are you envious of Marian, Catherine ?

CATHERINE.   Why, I have never even met Mr Townsend.

MRS PENNIMAN.   Oh, no, no.   I didn't mean that.   I mean, shouldn't you like to be an engaged girl, too ?

CATHERINE.   I don't know.   The question has never come up.

MRS PENNIMAN.   Not even in your own mind ?   Don't you ever think about having your own home and husband and children ?

CATHERINE (*very quietly*).   Yes, I think about it.

MRS PENNIMAN.   Well, don't you desire it ?

CATHERINE (*hesitantly*).   It is the *person* I think of.   It is, to find someone to love.

MRS PENNIMAN.   And someone who loves you.

CATHERINE (*simply*).   But that is the same thing.

(*There is a moment's pause.* SLOPER *enters, descends the stairs and comes into the room.*)

SLOPER.   Ah, Catherine.   (*He moves* C.)

(CATHERINE *rises and moves to the fireplace.*)

Good evening, my dear.

CATHERINE.   Good evening, Father.   Do you like my dress ?

SLOPER (*eyeing her fully*).   Is it possible this magnificent person is my daughter ?

(CATHERINE *does not know quite how to take this.*)

You are sumptuous, opulent—you look as if you had eighty thousand dollars a year.

CATHERINE.   I thought you would like the colour.

SLOPER.   Hm'm !

CATHERINE.   It is cherry red.

SLOPER. Ah'a!

CATHERINE. My mother used to wear it.

MRS PENNIMAN. In her hair ribbons.

SLOPER. Oh, yes, Catherine, but your mother was dark. *She* dominated the colour. (*He picks up the newspaper from the table* C.)

(CATHERINE *takes her embroidery out of the bag on the chair down* L., *sits down* L. *and commences to sew.* MRS PENNIMAN, *sensing tension, tries to mend matters.*)

MRS PENNIMAN. Catherine was at a meeting of the Ladies' Hospital Committee today, Austin.

SLOPER. Oh, really?

MRS PENNIMAN. She has been very active there all the week.

SLOPER. Good! (*To* CATHERINE.) How do you like it, my dear?

CATHERINE. Very much. It is very stimulating.

SLOPER. That's fine. I like women who do things. What is your particular duty?

CATHERINE. I copy out the vegetable lists for the children's ward.

SLOPER (*moving to the armchair*). Well, that's necessary work. (*He indicates the embroidery.*) Are you starting another of those samplers?

CATHERINE. Why, yes, Father. I find it a most agreeable pastime.

SLOPER. Don't let it turn into a life work, Catherine. (*He sits in the armchair and begins to read.*)

MRS PENNIMAN (*again stepping into the breach*). Catherine had such an amusing experience at the Hospital today, Austin. (*To* CATHERINE.) Catherine, dear, tell your father about that young woman. Tell him just the way you told me.

SLOPER (*with an expectant smile*). Yes, please do.

CATHERINE. Well—er—there was a young woman—er—also on the Committee and she asked me about veal.

SLOPER. Yes?

CATHERINE. She didn't know what it was.

SLOPER. I see?

MRS PENNIMAN (*eagerly*). She thought it was part of the cow, didn't she, Catherine?

CATHERINE. Yes—she didn't know it was calf.

SLOPER. She didn't?

CATHERINE (*struggling*). She didn't know any of the cuts of beef.

SLOPER (*waiting*). I see?

MRS PENNIMAN. You see, Austin, Catherine told her it was a *young* cow.

SLOPER. Yes?

CATHERINE (*lost*). Well, I just thought—she might not have liked it.

SLOPER. Ah! (*He indicates* CATHERINE'S *position.*) That is not a very good light for sewing, Catherine, you might hurt your eyes.

(*A carriage is heard approaching.*)

CATHERINE. Yes, Father.

(*The carriage stops. The doorbell rings.* MARIA *enters* L., *crosses to the front door and opens it.*)

MRS PENNIMAN (*rising*). Here they are.

(*She goes into the hall and stands below the hall table.* SLOPER *rises and puts his newspaper on the table up* L. CATHERINE *puts her sewing in the bag then rises, moves to* SLOPER *and stands below him,* L. *of the doors up* C., *with her arm in his.*)

MARIA (*at the front door*). Good evening, Mrs Almond.

(MRS ELIZABETH ALMOND, *a handsome woman in her forties, enters by the front door.*)

MRS ALMOND (*as she enters*). Good evening, Maria.

(MARIA *takes* MRS ALMOND'S *cape.*)

(*She crosses to* MRS PENNIMAN.) Livvie!

MRS PENNIMAN. Lizzie! (*She kisses* MRS ALMOND.)

(MARIAN ALMOND *enters by the front door.*)

MARIA. Good evening, Miss Marian.

MARIAN (*as she enters*). Good evening, Maria.

(MARIA *takes* MARIAN'S *shawl.* MRS ALMOND *enters the room.* MARIAN *moves to* MRS PENNIMAN *and kisses her.* ARTHUR TOWNSEND *and* MORRIS TOWNSEND *enter by the front door.* MARIA *takes* ARTHUR'S *hat and stick.* MORRIS *closes the front door.* ARTHUR *moves to* MARIAN *who introduces him to* MRS PENNIMAN, *and he kisses her hand.*)

MRS ALMOND. Good evening, Austin. Hello, Catherine, dear.

SLOPER. How nice to see you, Liz. (*He kisses her.*)

MRS ALMOND (*easing down* R.C.). Well, Austin, who's ill? Who's dead? Whom have you been cutting up lately?

(MORRIS *gives his hat and stick to* MARIA. MARIA *puts the clothes in the clothes closet.* ARTHUR *and* MARIAN *enter the room, arm in arm.* MORRIS *bows to* MRS PENNIMAN, *who curtsies, but does not speak.*)

SLOPER (*amused*). I see you are in good health, Liz. You're more respectful to me when your gout's troubling you.

(*The carriage is heard to depart.*)

Mrs Almond.   Arthur, this is my brother, Dr Sloper.

(Arthur *bows*.   Mrs Penniman *enters the room, moves down* r. *of
the couch and sits on the downstage end of it*.)

And this is Marian's cousin, Catherine.   (*She sits on the couch,
above* Mrs Penniman.)

Arthur.   How do you do, Miss Sloper?

(Morris *enters the room*.)

Marian.   Good evening, Uncle Austin.

Sloper.   Marian, my dear.   (*He kisses her*.)   How nice to see
you.

(Marian *crosses to* Catherine *and kisses her*.   Maria *moves
from the clothes closet, and closes the sliding doors before she
exits*.)

Marian.   Hello, Cathie.

Catherine.   Good evening, Marian.

(Marian *moves down* l.)

Arthur (*shaking hands with* Sloper).   How do you do,
Doctor?   I have taken the liberty of bringing my cousin.   I
thought that since you were meeting me, you would not mind
meeting him.   (*He turns to* Morris.)   Morris, meet Dr Sloper.
Dr Sloper—Morris Townsend.

Morris.   How do you do, sir?   (*He shakes hands with*
Sloper.)

Mrs Penniman.   And *I* am the doctor's other sister.

Morris (*turning and bowing*).   How do you do, ma'am?   I
hope you will pardon my intrusion on a family party, Dr and
Miss Sloper.   I am newly returned from Europe and feel somewhat lost.

Sloper.   I am delighted to meet you, sir.   (*To* Arthur.)
You did quite right to bring your cousin.

(Arthur *moves down* r. *of the couch*.)

Marian.   How grand you look, Cathie.   I told Morris he
should find you very grand, and then he was determined to
come.

Arthur (*beckoning to* Marian).   Marian.

Catherine.   Thank you, Marian.

(Marian *crosses to* Arthur *and sits down* r.   *There is a pause*.
Sloper *pats* Catherine's *hand*.   *She mistakes his meaning,
and curtsies to* Morris *and* Arthur.)

How do you do, sir?   How do you do, sir?

Sloper.   No, Catherine.   (*He loosens her hand from his arm*.)
The young gentlemen cannot take chairs until you do.

CATHERINE. I'm sorry, Father. (*She moves down* L. *and sits.*)

(SLOPER *indicates the stool up* C. *to* MORRIS, *who brings it from behind the table to front of it.* ARTHUR *puts the desk chair near* MARIAN *and sits.*)

MARIAN. Uncle Austin, Arthur says that a house in Washington Square is the best investment in the City.

SLOPER (*to* ARTHUR). I am happy to see that we think alike, sir.

ARTHUR. Er—yes—the counting house with which I am associated thinks very highly of the Square. We have funds available for mortgages at all times.

SLOPER. Well—that's most reassuring. (*He sits in the armchair.*)

MRS PENNIMAN. And when is the marriage to be, Marian?

MARIAN. The twentieth of November, Aunt Lavinia. Arthur wanted to hold me off till Spring, but I wouldn't have it. (*She puts her hand out to* ARTHUR.)

MORRIS. Arthur will have the truest cause to celebrate Thanksgiving of his life.

MRS PENNIMAN. How charmingly expressed, Mr Townsend.

MORRIS (*to* CATHERINE). I hear from Miss Almond that you are to be one of the bridesmaids, Miss Sloper.

MARIAN. Bridesmaid! Why, Cathie's to be my maid-of-honour.

MRS PENNIMAN. Perhaps Catherine will catch the bride's bouquet.

MRS ALMOND. Of course she will. Marian will aim it at Catherine. They can practise with a bean bag.

(*There is some polite laughter.* CATHERINE *nervously twists her handkerchief.* SLOPER *rises, moves to* CATHERINE, *takes the handkerchief from her and puts it in his pocket.*)

SLOPER (*giving* CATHERINE *a cue*). Mr Morris Townsend has lately returned from Europe, Catherine.

CATHERINE (*to* MORRIS). Have you been away long, sir?

MORRIS. Yes, I have, to my disadvantage as I now see.

CATHERINE. Why?

(SLOPER *sits in the armchair.*)

MORRIS. I find I have missed some lovely things at home.

CATHERINE. Oh!

MORRIS. Besides, people forget you.

MARIAN (*teasing*). He wants us to say that we would never forget him, don't you, Morris?

CATHERINE (*protesting*). Oh, Marian!

MORRIS (*smiling*). There is nothing I would rather hear. (*To*

CATHERINE.) Are you as great a tease as your cousin, Miss Sloper?

CATHERINE. No. (*She rises and starts to move up* C.)

(MORRIS *and* ARTHUR *rise.* SLOPER *rises and bars* CATHERINE'S *way.*)

SLOPER. Is there something I can get you, Catherine?

CATHERINE (*trapped*). My embroidery . . .

SLOPER. We will admire it later, my dear.

(CATHERINE *resumes her seat down* L.)

MORRIS. Ah, Miss Sloper, you are just like the young ladies of Paris. They, too, are always busy with their *petit-point*. (*He pronounces the last word with a good French accent.*)

MRS PENNIMAN (*ecstatically*). Oh! You speak French.

MORRIS. A little, ma'am.

SLOPER. Did you make the Grand Tour, Mr Townsend?

MORRIS. No, sir. I spent most of my time in France and Italy.

MRS PENNIMAN. Italy! Oh, how beautiful it must be!

MORRIS. You don't know it, ma'am?

(SLOPER *sits in the armchair.*)

MRS PENNIMAN. No, I've never been there, but I have always felt it must be the most romantic country. Such handsome men —(*hastily*) and such beautiful women. Tell me, Mr Townsend, do you find our American young ladies very different?

MORRIS. So different, ma'am. (*He looks expressively at* CATHERINE.) So delightfully different! (*He bows.*)

(*In a spasm of nervousness,* CATHERINE *knocks the miniature off the table against her right elbow.*)

SLOPER (*half-rising*). It's all right, Catherine.

CATHERINE (*picking up the miniature*). I didn't break it, Father. (*She replaces it on the table.*)

(MORRIS *resumes his seat on the stool.*)

SLOPER (*calming her*). Of course you didn't, my dear. (*Then quickly, in order to draw away the attention.*) Mr Townsend, I suppose I shall find Paris unchanged?

MORRIS. Are you planning a trip, sir?

SLOPER. I hope to attend a medical congress there this winter.

MRS ALMOND. It's a tremendous trip, Austin, just to go and talk to a lot of other doctors.

SLOPER (*smiling*). Oh, between talks I shall find time for other things. I shall walk in every street I walked in the first time many years ago; I shall shop in every shop . . .

Morris. And smell every smell!

(*They all laugh.*)

I see you really love the city, sir.

Sloper. I have good reason to—I went there on my wedding trip.

Marian. We have been having a wonderful time listening to all the new French songs. We kept Morris playing for hours last evening.

Morris. I don't know how you stood it!

Arthur. Oh, come now, Morris, (*he claps his hands*) don't be modest!

Marian. Would you like to hear some, Cathie?

(Catherine *does not answer.*)

Mrs Penniman. I should love to.

Arthur (*looking around*). Too bad, Morris, no pianoforte.

Morris (*gaily*). Oh, what a pity! (*Confidentially, to* Catherine.) And it's my trump card, Miss Sloper.

Mrs Penniman. There is a spinet in the study.

Catherine (*appalled*). But that was mother's!

Sloper (*rising*). The instrument is not in tune.

Morris. I do not play well enough, sir, for that to make much difference.

Sloper (*firmly*). I'm sorry.

Mrs Almond. Let them try it, Austin. I haven't heard music here in a long time.

Mrs Penniman (*rising and crossing to* Sloper). Please, Austin.

Arthur (*moving below the couch*). He wants to outshine me, Doctor, with the ladies.

Sloper. Very well, Lavinia, if you wish it.

Mrs Penniman (*moving to the door down* L.). This way, Mr Townsend.

(Morris *rises, crosses to the door down* L. *and opens it.* Mrs Penniman *exits down* L. Morris *stands down* L. *of the door.* Marian *rises and crosses with* Arthur *to the door down* L.)

Marian. Let us use some of our wedding money for a fine pianoforte, Arthur.

(Arthur *and* Marian *exit down* L. *A low hum of conversation is heard off down* L. *whenever the door is open.* Mrs Penniman *re-enters down* L.)

Mrs Penniman. Catherine, dear, bring the lamp. There is none on the spinet.

(*She exits down* L. Catherine *rises, crosses to the desk and picks up the lamp from it.* Morris *crosses quickly to* Catherine.)

MORRIS. Please allow me, Miss Sloper. It might be too heavy for you.

(CATHERINE *tries to keep hold of the lamp as* MORRIS *tries to relieve her of it.*)

CATHERINE. Oh, no !
MORRIS. Please . . .
CATHERINE. It's quite all right.
SLOPER (*smiling*). Catherine ! Let the young man carry it for you.
CATHERINE (*relinquishing the lamp*). Yes, Father.
MORRIS (*crossing with the lamp to the door down* L.). You thought I was going to drop it, didn't you, Miss Sloper ? I *won't*. I shall be most careful.

(CATHERINE *crosses to the door down* L. *and exits.* MORRIS *follows her off and closes the door.*)

SLOPER. I shall never understand it. Her mother was so graceful.

(MRS ALMOND, *embarrassed, looks away.* MRS PENNIMAN *enters down* L.)

MRS PENNIMAN. Austin, Mr Townsend can't open the spinet. Is it locked ?
SLOPER (*taking a small key from his watch-chain*). Here is the key, Lavinia. See that I get it back. (*He hands the key to* MRS PENNIMAN.)
MRS PENNIMAN. Thank you. (*She turns in the doorway. Confidentially.*) Isn't he charming ?

(MRS PENNIMAN *exits down* L. *and closes the door behind her.*)

SLOPER. She does *not* mean Arthur, Elizabeth.
MRS ALMOND. I know she doesn't.
SLOPER. What about this cousin ? Who is he ? (*He takes a cigar from the box on the table* L. *of the armchair.*)
MRS ALMOND. He's a *distant* cousin, it seems. Arthur's mother is always talking about branches of the family ; elder branches, younger branches, inferior branches, as if it were a royal house. Now, Arthur, it appears, is on the royal line ; his cousin Morris is not.
SLOPER. Cousin Morris has a royal ease about inviting himself along, hasn't he ? Quite the sort of figure to please the ladies.
MRS ALMOND. Yes.
SLOPER. Did he do anything before he went on his travels ?
MRS ALMOND. I don't think so. I believe he had a very small inheritance. He intimated that he had used it up. He lives in the Second Avenue with his sister.

SLOPER. Who is she? (*He takes the box of matches from the mantelpiece.*)

MRS ALMOND. A Mrs Montgomery, a nice little woman, a widow. I met her once at a charity bazaar for needy children. She has five of her own.

SLOPER. A widow, with five children? Do you mean he lives *on* her?

MRS ALMOND. I can hardly answer that, Austin. You would have to ask her.

(*The church clock strikes three-quarters.* SLOPER *lights a match.*)

Tell me—what do you think of Arthur?

SLOPER (*smiling*). Arthur? Well, he isn't very lively, is he? I see him as the president of a bank at fifty.

MRS ALMOND. Good!

SLOPER. A small bank. (*He lights his cigar.*)

MRS ALMOND. Even so, Marian will like that.

SLOPER. Are you entirely satisfied with the arrangement?

MRS ALMOND (*shrugging*). She wanted him.

SLOPER (*pacing down* L.). Do you suppose there is another Arthur somewhere in this great city of ours?

MRS ALMOND. Catherine will find a husband.

SLOPER. You think so?

MRS ALMOND. She has the prospect of thirty thousand dollars a year.

SLOPER (*moving* C.; *with a smile*). I see that you appreciate her.

MRS ALMOND. I don't mean that's her only merit. You always have a way of alluding to her as an unmarriageable girl.

SLOPER. You see how she is with young men.

MRS ALMOND. That is the trouble in New York; the men are too young. They marry at the age of innocence, before the age of calculation. If they only waited a little, Catherine would fare better.

SLOPER. As a calculation? Thank you very much! (*He turns to the fire.*)

MRS ALMOND. Of course I didn't mean it that way.

SLOPER (*shrugging*). We need not deceive each other, my dear.

MRS ALMOND (*rising and moving* C.). Austin, are you really as detached as you seem about Catherine?

(SLOPER *puts his cigar in the ashtray on the mantelpiece and turns.*)

SLOPER. Detached? That's the last thing I am. (*He moves to the table* C.) I am deeply interested in every phase of her life. Detached! I wish I were.

MRS ALMOND. Why? (*She sits on the stool* C.)

SLOPER (*pouring out a glass of sherry*). Because I wish I had

confidence in her ability to manage herself, and her future, with
some wisdom, or even some intelligence.

MRS ALMOND.   I see that you have no confidence and I imagine
Catherine sees it, too.

SLOPER.   If you are reproaching me, Liz, you must be more
specific.   (*He hands the glass to her.*)   What would you like me to
do for her that I haven't done ?   Is there something I have
missed ?   She has been to the best schools in the city.   She
has had the finest training I could get her in music and dancing.
She has sat here with me evenings on end, and I have tried to
make conversation with her, and give her some social adeptness.
She has never been constrained in the spending of money, or
in the direction of the household.   I have given her freedom
wherever I could.   The result is what you see—an entirely
mediocre and defenceless creature with not a shred of poise.
What did I do wrong, my dear sister ?   If you know, I wish
you'd tell me, for *I* do not.

MRS ALMOND (*placing her glass on the table* C.).   I do not
mean that you have not done your duty as a father.

SLOPER.   I have been as good a father as it was possible for
me to be with the material Providence gave me.

(*Three running chords are heard on a spinet off down* L.   SLOPER
and MRS ALMOND *listen for a moment.*)

MRS ALMOND (*surprised*).   Why, it *is* in tune, Arthur.

SLOPER (*moving to the fireplace*).   Yes.   (*He picks up his cigar.*)

(*A voice, presumably* MORRIS, *is heard off down* L. *singing " Chan-
son de Fortunio ".*)

MRS ALMOND.   That's quite remarkable, after all these years.

SLOPER (*sitting in the armchair*).   I keep it looked after.   I
have a man who comes in three or four times a year.

MRS ALMOND.   You should encourage Catherine to play.

SLOPER.   I do.   She can't.

MRS ALMOND.   Austin, you are so intolerant !   And you
expect so much.

SLOPER.   Yes, I expect everything.   You remember her
mother, Liz.   Her mother who had so much grace and gaiety.
(*He looks at the miniature.*)   Her mother who was such a pleasure
to look at and be with.   This is her child.   (*He pauses.*)   I was
entitled to expect that some day she should make it up to me,
wasn't I ?

MRS ALMOND.   Make what up ?

SLOPER.   Her mother's death !   She killed her mother in
getting born.

MRS ALMOND (*pityingly*).   Oh, Austin !

(*The song finishes.   The sound of applause is heard off down* L.)

SLOPER.   I've lived these years in loneliness, waiting for

Catherine to be all the lovely things her mother was. I let nothing interfere with it. I didn't marry. I didn't do anything to endanger the process. I concentrated my life on seeing her approach the perfection of her mother.

MRS ALMOND. No child could compete with this image you have of her mother. You have idealized that poor dead woman beyond all human recognition.

SLOPER. You are not entitled to say that. Only *I* know what I lost when she died.

(*The voice off down* L. *is heard to commence singing a second song, " Plaisir d'Amour ".* SLOPER *and* MRS ALMOND *listen for a few moments.* MRS ALMOND *watches* SLOPER.)

(*He rises.*) When I hear that spinet played, (*he paces down* L. *and turns*) I remember the day she got it. (*He paces up* L.C.) We were in Paris, (*he turns*) and bought it at *Pleyel's*. She wouldn't sail for home until she found a captain who was willing to let her take it on board with her. Six months later she was dead.

MRS ALMOND (*gently*). That was a long time ago, Austin.

SLOPER (*moving to the fire ; with his back to* MRS ALMOND). That is no consolation.

They listen to the song as—

the CURTAIN *falls.*

SCENE 2

SCENE.—*The same. An afternoon two weeks later.*
   The couch is now down R.C., *facing down stage. There is an oblong table above it. The chair from down* R. *is near the* R. *end of the couch. The table from* C. *has been removed and the stool has been placed in the bay of the upstage window.*
   (*See the Ground Plan and Photograph of the Scene.*)

When the CURTAIN *rises the room is brilliant with the sunlight from the Square, and there is an Indian Summer quality in the light which makes the room seem very cheerful. A bright fire burns in the grate.* MRS PENNIMAN *is seated on the couch.* MORRIS *is seated* R.

MRS PENNIMAN (*laughing*). Really, Mr Townsend, you shouldn't make fun of Arthur. After all, he is your relative.

MORRIS. I don't care about that ! But he did introduce me into this house, and for that I must be grateful all the rest of my life. (*He bows his head to her gracefully.*) Here I have found a true friend.

MRS PENNIMAN. Perhaps you have found something more important than that in this house.

MORRIS. Did you tell her that I would call today ?

MRS PENNIMAN. No, I must confess I did not. She is so gentle, so timid, I was afraid she would take flight at your third visit within the week.

MORRIS (*rising and moving above the couch to* L.). There's nothing special about three visits, is there ? (*He looks at his watch.*) And since she's out anyway, what have we gained ?

(*The church clock strikes four.*)

MRS PENNIMAN. She will be home, I am sure of it.

MORRIS. Well, but when ?

MRS PENNIMAN (*pleased with his impatience*). Ah, Mr Townsend, you remind me so of the Reverend Penniman. The same ardency, the same passionate nature.

MORRIS (*easing* C.). Was she pleased with the flowers, Mrs Penniman ?

MRS PENNIMAN. I think very pleased.

MORRIS. What did she say ?

MRS PENNIMAN. She said, " They are a spring flower. It is unusual to get them so late."

MORRIS. Is that all ?

MRS PENNIMAN. But she took them upstairs to her sitting-room and placed them right next to her chair at the window. I think that's good, don't you ?

MORRIS. What did her father say ?

MRS PENNIMAN. How do you mean ?

MORRIS. Did he tease her when he saw them ?

MRS PENNIMAN. How would he see them ? He never goes into her sitting-room.

MORRIS (*pumping*). Does Catherine—I mean, Miss Sloper . . .

MRS PENNIMAN (*smiling*). My boy, you may let yourself go when you are with me. (*She eases along the couch seat to the* R. *end of it.*)

MORRIS (*sitting on the couch,* L. *of her*). Does Catherine see many young men, Mrs Penniman ?

MRS PENNIMAN (*embarrassed*). Er—well, she receives many invitations. And she always attends the Cotillions.

MORRIS. I don't mean that. I mean does she receive young men like myself, often ?

MRS PENNIMAN. She is of a retiring nature.

MORRIS. I cannot believe that she is so reserved with everybody. I am afraid she disapproves of me.

MRS PENNIMAN (*in alarm*). Oh, no !

MORRIS. She gives me no encouragement.

MRS PENNIMAN. But that is because she is so shy.

MORRIS. Oh dear, then we shall never know her heart, shall we ?

MRS PENNIMAN. But she is not shy with *me*, Mr Townsend.

She confides in me freely. In the privacy of her own room she is most expressive.

MORRIS. Dare I ask what my name has brought forth in that privacy ?

MRS PENNIMAN. I can assure you that she has a wealth of feeling, but she is wary of showing it.

MORRIS (*musing*). It's odd. In Europe, a girl like that would have been married long since. Why, in Paris with her income she might have got a Count.

MRS PENNIMAN (*enchanted*). A Count ? Do you really think so ? (*Thoughtfully*.) But Austin would never have it.

MORRIS. Tell me about the doctor, ma'am. What are his interests ? Does he like art, or music ? Has he any hobby ?

MRS PENNIMAN. His work is his hobby. Medicine is his only mistress.

MORRIS. That's a devil of a difficult thing for a man like me to talk about.

MRS PENNIMAN. Once he knows what is going on in your heart, you will have plenty to talk about between you.

(CATHERINE *enters by the front door*. MORRIS *rises and moves to the fireplace*.)

(*She calls*.) Catherine, is that you ?
CATHERINE (*off*). Yes, Aunt.

(CATHERINE *comes into the room. She carries a very small packet*.)

MRS PENNIMAN. You have a visitor, young lady. He has been waiting for your return most anxiously.

CATHERINE (*with a curtsy to* MORRIS). Good afternoon.

MORRIS. It is a beautiful afternoon for me now, Miss Sloper. But I was afraid you might not come back at all.

CATHERINE. Oh, I should have to come back some time. (*She puts the packet on the table*.) I live here.

MORRIS (*smiling*). I know you do, Miss Sloper. That's why I am here.

(*There is a slight pause*.)

MRS PENNIMAN. Mr Townsend wondered if his flowers had been delivered in good condition.

CATHERINE. Yes, thank you. They were very fresh. I mailed a note to you this morning.

MORRIS. I shall treasure it, Miss Sloper, although I did not send the flowers in order to be thanked. I sent them to give you pleasure.

CATHERINE. Thank you.

MORRIS (*feeling in his pockets*). Oh, I found the poem I told you about.

CATHERINE. Did you ?

MORRIS. I am such a vagabond—I've left it in my hat. (*He moves up* C.) Pardon me, ma'am. I'll get it.

(*He goes into the hall and then into the clothes closet.*)

MRS PENNIMAN (*rising and coming to* L. *of* CATHERINE). I will leave you alone with him.
CATHERINE. What will I talk about?

(MRS PENNIMAN *takes off* CATHERINE'S *bonnet, then her wrap.*)

MRS PENNIMAN (*smiling*). You will not have to do the talking. My dear child, he has come a-courting.
CATHERINE. Do you mean courting me?
MRS PENNIMAN. Certainly not me, miss! (*She takes* CATHERINE'S *parasol.*) You must be very gracious to him.

(MORRIS *re-enters up* C. *He carries a sheet of paper with the poem written on it.*)

MORRIS (R. *of* CATHERINE). I copied it off late last night. (*He looks expressively at* CATHERINE.) I was restless and could not sleep.
MRS PENNIMAN (*moving up* C.). Mr Townsend, you must excuse me. I have numerous duties which call me. I trust that we shall see you again.
MORRIS (*bowing low*). I am your servant, ma'am.

(CATHERINE *takes off her gloves.*)

MRS PENNIMAN (*turning in the hall*). Catherine, don't forget to rest before going out, for tonight. (*To* MORRIS.) Our girl is off to another of her endless parties, Mr Townsend! Dancing—dancing till dawn!

(*She exits up the stairs.*)

MORRIS. It makes me very unhappy to hear that.
CATHERINE. What?
MORRIS. That you are so gay, so sought after. It makes my way harder.
CATHERINE. Oh, but I am not going to a party tonight. My father and I are dining with Mr and Mrs Hone. That is all.
MORRIS. That's what I like about you, you are so honest Will you tell me something, Miss Sloper? Did you go out today because you thought I might call?
CATHERINE (*after a pause*). Yes.
MORRIS. Do you not like to see me?
CATHERINE. Yes, I like to see you, Mr Townsend. But you have called so frequently this week that I . . .
MORRIS (*smiling*). That you are tired of me.
CATHERINE. No.
MORRIS. You consider my behaviour improper?

CATHERINE. I do not know. I am puzzled.

MORRIS (*laughing*). Good! I like that! If you are puzzled, you are thinking of me, and that is what I want above all; that you should think of me.

CATHERINE (*moving below the couch*). Mr Townsend, you are very bold. (*She puts her gloves on the sofa table.*)

MORRIS (*confidently*). I will be bolder; I will ask you one more question. Miss Sloper, when you came back just now, did you—hope that I would be gone—or—that I would be here?

CATHERINE (*half turning to him*). Is that the poem?

MORRIS (*moving to her; gaily*). It is! I had forgotten it. I forget everything when I find myself here with you. It says the things I tried to say to you last time I was here.

CATHERINE (*taking the paper*). May I read it? (*She eases down R.*)

MORRIS. Oh, not now! Perhaps you will read it when you are alone. It will say more to you then. I will think of you reading it when I stand under your window.

CATHERINE (*turning*). Oh, Mr Townsend, you must not do that!

MORRIS (*mocking her gently*). Oh, Miss Sloper, how am I to help doing it? I think of you constantly.

CATHERINE. I am not very good at this kind of conversation.

MORRIS. Neither am I. I am afraid that is our trouble—I am not a glib man, Miss Sloper.

CATHERINE. Oh, but I think you talk very well! (*She sits on the chair down R.*)

MORRIS (*sitting on the couch*). Never when I need it most, never when I am with you. Oh, when I'm with Mrs Penniman, or in my room at home, I can think of the most delightful things to say—can you understand that?

CATHERINE (*smiling*). Yes, I can.

MORRIS. But here, with you, I sound like a fool.

CATHERINE. I don't think so.

MORRIS. Well, if ever you should think so, if ever I have sounded high-flown or false, put it down to that, will you?

CATHERINE. I will try.

MORRIS. And take pity on my situation.

CATHERINE. What situation?

MORRIS. Miss Sloper, I have fallen in love with you.

CATHERINE (*with a gasp*). You have?

MORRIS. You are breathless.

CATHERINE. Yes, I am.

MORRIS. Why—is it so strange?

CATHERINE. Yes, it is very strange.

(SLOPER *enters by the front door and moves to the foot of the stairs. He carries his walking-stick, gloves and medical bag. He puts*

*the walking-stick in the vase, and his hat and gloves on the hall
table.* CATHERINE *rises and crosses down* L. MORRIS *rises and
moves to* R. *of the table above the couch.*)

SLOPER (*in the hall*). Ah, Catherine, you are receiving ?
CATHERINE. Yes, Father. I have a visitor.

(SLOPER *enters the room bringing his bag with him.*)

SLOPER. Good afternoon, my dear. How do you do, Mr
Townsend ? (*He shakes hands, above the table, with* MORRIS.)
MORRIS. Good afternoon, Dr Sloper.
SLOPER (*looking around*). Is your cousin here with you ? (*To*
CATHERINE.) Where's the happy couple ? (*He moves* C.)
CATHERINE (*moving to* SLOPER *and taking his bag*). They are
not here, Father. (*She puts the bag on the chair down* L.)

(*The church clock strikes the quarter.*)

MORRIS (*moving to* L. *of the sofa table*). I took the liberty of
coming on my own, sir. I wanted to thank Miss Sloper and
yourself for having received me the first time.
SLOPER. That's most polite, sir. It was a very small gathering, and we were pleased to have you.
MORRIS (*gracefully*). Sometimes it is the small parties at
which one takes the greatest pleasure. This one gave me an
excuse to call on a most attractive young lady, and her attractive
father.
SLOPER. Oh, we are not that attractive. Catherine, pull the
bell, will you. I'd like my sherry and biscuits.

(CATHERINE *moves up* L.C., *pulls the bell, then stares out towards
the upstage window.*)

Mr Townsend might enjoy some with me.
MORRIS (*crossing to the fire*). I'd be honoured. (*He smooths
his hair.*)
SLOPER (*sniffing*). That's an excellent bay rum you are using,
Mr Townsend.
MORRIS. I brought it with me from France, Doctor. Permit
me to share it with you.
SLOPER. Why in the world should you ?
MORRIS. There is no reason, sir, except the pleasure it would
give me.
SLOPER. I could hardly allow you to do that. (*He sits in the
armchair.*) Well, Catherine.

(CATHERINE *does not hear.*)

Catherine ! (*He claps his hands.*) What have you been up to,
my dear ? Did you decide to do anything further about the
music lessons ?

CATHERINE (*moving* C.).   Yes, Father, I called on Mr Rougini after lunch.

SLOPER.   And what did he say?

CATHERINE.   He said the harp was a very difficult instrument.

SLOPER.   Well, we both know that, my dear.   What else did he say?

CATHERINE.   He did not think I was suited to it.

SLOPER.   Why not?

CATHERINE (*timidly*).   You need a true ear for the harp.   It seems that I have not a very true ear.

SLOPER.   Nonsense, my dear—that's impossible!   Your mother's ear was impeccable.   Why, she used to tune her own pianoforte.

CATHERINE (*moving below the couch*).   Yes, Father, I know.

MORRIS (*tactfully*).   Miss Sloper has a great appreciation for music surely.   That is a sufficient talent in itself.

SLOPER.   Do you find it so?

(MARIA *enters up* C. *from* L.   *She carries a tray with sherry and biscuits.*   CATHERINE *sits on the couch.*   MORRIS *lifts the bag off the chair down* L., *puts the bag on the floor, then sits.*)

(*He rises.*)   Good afternoon, Maria.

MARIA (R. *of* SLOPER).   Good afternoon, Doctor.

SLOPER.   Is Cook's knee any better?

MARIA.   It is a little easier, Doctor.

(SLOPER *takes the stopper out of the decanter, puts it on the tray then picks up the decanter and the other glass.*)

SLOPER (*filling the glass on the tray*).   I'll be up to see her in a little while.   Here, give this to Mr Townsend.   (*He fills the glass he is holding for himself.*)

(MARIA *takes the glass on the tray to* MORRIS *then moves to* L. *of* SLOPER.)

MARIA.   She's not upstairs, Doctor, she's in the kitchen.

SLOPER (*putting the decanter on the tray*).   This is hopeless, Maria!   How am I to get rid of the inflammation unless you keep her in bed?   (*He replaces the stopper in the decanter.*)

MARIA.   Perhaps you'll talk to her, Doctor.

SLOPER.   I'll be down to see her as soon as I finish this.

MARIA.   Thank you, sir.

(*She moves above* SLOPER, *puts the tray on the table above the couch, then exits up* C. *to* L.   SLOPER *moves to the fireplace.*)

MORRIS.   You are a very kind man, sir.   Most great doctors are too busy to see the illness under their noses.

SLOPER.   Mr Townsend, you are full of agreeable and flattering cbservations, both for Catherine and myself. I wonder why ? (*He sits in the armchair.*)

MORRIS. That is the way you both strike me, sir. I told Miss Sloper earlier—I am very candid. (*He drinks.*)

CATHERINE (*to* SLOPER). Yes, he is very candid.

(SLOPER *looks at* CATHERINE, *then at* MORRIS.)

SLOPER. How do you keep busy since your return to New York, Mr Townsend ? Are you looking for a position ?

MORRIS. Oh, " position " is more than I should presume to call it ! That sounds so fine. I should like some quiet work— anything to turn an honest penny.

SLOPER. What sort of thing should you prefer ? (*He drinks.*)

MORRIS. You mean what am I fitted for ? Very little, I am afraid. I have nothing but my good right arm, as they say in the melodramas.

SLOPER. You are too modest. In addition to your good right arm you have a very good mind. (*He puts his glass on the table* L.) I know nothing of you but what I see ; but I see that you are extremely intelligent.

CATHERINE (*murmuring*). Oh, yes—yes !

MORRIS (*rising, crossing to the sofa table and putting his glass on the tray*). I don't know what to answer when you say that. You advise me, then, not to despair ?

SLOPER (*with a smile*). I should be sorry to admit that a robust, well-disposed man need ever despair. If he doesn't suc- ceed in one thing, he can try another. Only, he should choose with discretion.

MORRIS. Ah, yes, with discretion. Well, I have been indis- creet formerly, but I think I have got over it. I am very steady now. (*He smiles.*) Were you kindly intending to propose some- thing to my advantage ?

SLOPER. No, I have no particular proposal to make. But occasionally one hears of opportunities. I hear, for instance, the West is opening up. Many young men are turning their eyes in that direction.

MORRIS (*crossing to the chair* L.). I'm afraid I shouldn't be able to manage that. I must seek my fortune here or nowhere. (*He sits.*) You see, I have ties here. (*To* CATHERINE.) I have a widowed sister from whom I have been separated for a long time, and to whom I am everything.

CATHERINE. Naturally.

MORRIS (*to* SLOPER ; *smiling*). I shouldn't know how to tell her that I must leave her. She depends on me so much.

SLOPER. That's very proper, family feeling is very proper. I think I've heard of your sister. (*He picks up his glass.*)

MORRIS. It is possible, though I rather doubt it ; she lives so very quietly.

SLOPER. As quietly, you mean, as a lady may who has several young children.

(MORRIS *laughs, rises and moves to the fireplace.*)

MORRIS. Yes, my nephews and nieces—that's the very point. I am helping to bring them up. I'm a sort of amateur tutor ; I give them lessons.

SLOPER. That's very proper, but it's hardly a career. (*He drinks.*)

MORRIS. No, it won't make my fortune.

SLOPER (*incisively*). Ah ! (*He rises.*) You must not be too much bent on a fortune. (*He puts his glass on the sofa table.*) But I will keep you in mind, Mr Townsend. Be sure I will not lose sight of you. (*He turns to* CATHERINE.) Catherine, I am going downstairs.

(CATHERINE *rises.* SLOPER *moves to get his bag and* MORRIS *hands it to him.*)

Oh, thank you. Good afternoon, Mr Townsend. (*He goes into the hall.*)

MORRIS. Good afternoon, Doctor. I am very grateful for your interest.

SLOPER (*turning in the hall*). Yes—yes, indeed.

(*He exits up* C. *to* L. *There is a pause.*)

MORRIS. He doesn't like me—he doesn't like me at all. Extraordinary man !

CATHERINE. I don't see why you should think that.

MORRIS. I feel ; I am very quick to feel.

CATHERINE. Oh, no ! I am sure you are mistaken.

MORRIS. Well, you ask him, and you will see.

CATHERINE (*slowly*). I would rather not ask him, if there is any danger of his saying what you think.

MORRIS (*moving to her*). It wouldn't give you any pleasure to contradict him ?

CATHERINE. I never contradict him.

MORRIS. Would you hear me abused without opening your lips in my defence ?

CATHERINE. Oh, he won't abuse you. He doesn't know you well enough.

(MORRIS *laughs.*)

I shall simply not mention you.

MORRIS. That is not what I should have liked you to say. I should have liked you to say, " If my father does not think well of you, what does it matter ? "

CATHERINE. But I couldn't say that ! It *would* matter.

MORRIS. Do you know, I believe you could ? I believe you could do anything for one whom you loved !

CATHERINE (*crossing down* L. *and standing with her back to him*). Mr Townsend, you mustn't speak to me in this way. I mustn't listen to this.

MORRIS (*moving close behind her and pleading passionately*). It is two weeks since first I saw you, and I have not had an easy moment since that night. I think of nothing else. I am possessed by you.

CATHERINE (*with her head down and with desperate sincerity*). How could you be? How could you?

MORRIS (*moving above and to* L. *of her*). My dearest girl, my whole life depends on your believing me, believing how much I care for you. You are everything I have ever yearned for in a woman.

CATHERINE (*looking up*). But I am so . . .

(*Before she can finish, he draws her to him and kisses her. After a moment her arms go round him tightly.*)

MORRIS. Will you marry me, Catherine?

CATHERINE (*looking at him fully, for the first time*). Yes.

MORRIS (*smiling at her*). You make me very happy. Do you love me?

CATHERINE. Yes.

MORRIS. Dear Catherine! (*He kisses her.*)

CATHERINE (*holding him*). I love you! I love you!

MORRIS. I will cherish you for ever.

CATHERINE (*detaching herself and crossing below the couch*). We must do our duty. We must speak to my father. I will speak to him this evening. You must speak to him tomorrow.

MORRIS (*moving to* L. *of her*). It is sweet of you to do it first. The young man, the happy lover, usually does that. But just as you please.

CATHERINE (*sitting on the couch*). Women are more tactful. (*She smiles bravely.*) They can persuade better.

MORRIS (*sitting* L. *of her on the couch and holding her hands*). You will need all your powers of persuasion. (*He looks at her.*) But then, you are irresistible!

CATHERINE. Morris, promise me one thing. When you speak to my father, you will be very respectful.

MORRIS. I shall try. I certainly would rather have you easily than have to fight for you.

CATHERINE. Do not speak of fighting; we shall not have to fight.

MORRIS. We must be prepared. After all, it's natural for your father to want a brilliant match for you; you have everything—position, wealth, and your own sweetness. And I am a poor man, Catherine.

CATHERINE. Oh, but my father will not mind that.

MORRIS. He might. He might fear that I am mercenary.

CATHERINE. Mercenary?

MORRIS. That I only want your money.

CATHERINE. Oh, no!

MORRIS. He may say it.

CATHERINE. But that is easily answered I should simply say that he is mistaken.

MORRIS. You must make a great point cf that, Catherine.

CATHERINE. Why?

MORRIS. Because it is from the fact of your having money that our difficulties are likely to come.

CATHERINE (drawing away from him momentarily). Morris, are you very sure you love me?

MORRIS (turning her face with his left hand). My own dearest, can you doubt it?

CATHERINE. I have only known it for five minutes, but now it seems that I could never do without it.

MORRIS. You shall never be called upon to try. Now, there is something you must tell me. (He pats her hand.) You must tell me that if your father is against me, if he even forbids our marriage, you will still be faithful, no matter what comes.

CATHERINE. Yes, Morris—no matter what comes.

MORRIS. You know you are your own mistress—you are of age.

CATHERINE. I love you. I will always love you.

MORRIS (kissing her hair). My dear girl. (He rises and eases up c.) Well, I must leave you now. But I will be back in the morning to call on him.

CATHERINE (rising and crossing to L. of him). Yes. At what time?

MORRIS. At eleven sharp.

CATHERINE. I will tell him. You will be punctual, Morris?

MORRIS (holding her hands). Never fear, my love! When I want something badly, I am on the dot. (He kisses her and goes into the hall.) Be your own sweet self, and you will melt him.

(He gets his hat from the clothes closet then exits by the front door. CATHERINE stands L.C., facing down stage, half-smiling and dazed. MRS PENNIMAN enters down the stairs and moves to R. of CATHERINE.)

MRS PENNIMAN. Oh, he has left! Catherine, is he not charming?

CATHERINE. Yes, Aunt. (She moves to the stairs.) I must go to my room.

MRS PENNIMAN (following her to R. of the stairs). Without telling me what he said?

CATHERINE. I must speak to my father.

MRS PENNIMAN. But, Catherine, I am your natural confidante.

CATHERINE. Yes, Aunt, but I must speak to my father first.
I promised Morris I would.

MRS PENNIMAN. Oh, you call him Morris now !

CATHERINE. Yes, Aunt, I call him Morris now.

(SLOPER *enters the hall from* R. *He carries his bag.*)

SLOPER. Ah, Catherine, has our guest taken his leave ?

CATHERINE. Yes, Father. Is Cook's knee better ?

SLOPER. Somewhat.

CATHERINE (*with resolution*). Father ! May I speak to you
privately in ten minutes ?

SLOPER (*with humour*). Yes, I think I could make such an
engagement.

CATHERINE. I will be down promptly.

(*She exits up the stairs.* SLOPER *stares after her.* MRS PENNIMAN
moves to the couch and sits.)

SLOPER (*moving* C.). Well, Lavinia ! Did you know that we
had a caller ? (*He puts his bag on the floor* R. *of the armchair.*)

MRS PENNIMAN. Why, my dear, you can't see the door for
him. He's been here *three* times this week.

SLOPER. Has he, indeed ?

MRS PENNIMAN. Yes. Isn't it wonderful ?

SLOPER. What's wonderful about it ?

MRS PENNIMAN. Why, Austin, be sensible. He is a charming
young man. I never dreamed that he'd be this interested in
Catherine.

SLOPER. Nor did I. Why hasn't Catherine told me about
these visits ?

MRS PENNIMAN. Well, I think she feared at first that it might
all come to nothing. But this afternoon when he and I were
alone together he spoke of her in terms that were unmistakable.
He is devoted to her.

SLOPER. What do you know of Mr Townsend ?

MRS PENNIMAN. He has told me a great deal about himself.
In fact, his whole history. I'm sure he will tell it all to you,
Austin, and you must listen to him kindly.

SLOPER. I think I shall request him very kindly to leave
Catherine alone.

MRS PENNIMAN (*surprised*). But why ? I'm sure his intentions are entirely honourable.

SLOPER. You think he is sincere ?

MRS PENNIMAN. Deeply sincere ! I can tell that by the
things he has told me ; he has bared his very soul to me.

SLOPER. Indeed. And revealed exactly what ?

MRS PENNIMAN. Well, he frankly confesses that he has been
wild. But he's paid for it, Austin.

SLOPER. Does that account for his impoverishment ?

MRS PENNIMAN. I don't simply mean in terms of money. He
is very much alone in the world.

SLOPER. Why ? He has a devoted sister, and half a dozen
nephews and nieces !

MRS PENNIMAN. The nephews and nieces are all children, and
the sister is not a very sympathetic person.

SLOPER. I hope he doesn't abuse her to you, for I am told he
lives on her.

MRS PENNIMAN (*rising*). Lives on her ?

SLOPER. Lives with her, and does nothing for himself ; it s
about the same thing.

MRS PENNIMAN. But he's looking for a position most
earnestly.

(SLOPER *turns away a little.*)

He hopes every day to find one.

SLOPER (*turning to her*). Do you suppose he's looking for it
here, Lavinia, in this front parlour ?

MRS PENNIMAN. What can you mean, Austin ?

SLOPER. Wouldn't the position of husband to a defenceless
young woman with a large fortune suit him to perfection ?

MRS PENNIMAN (*shocked*). Austin ! How can you entertain
such a suspicion ?

SLOPER. Suspicion ? (*He picks up his bag.*) It is a diagnosis,
my dear.

(*He exits down* L., *leaving the door open.*)

MRS PENNIMAN (*moving to* L. *of the door down* L.). You are
not in your clinic ! This is not a matter for diagnosis. You have
only to use your eyes, which are as good as mine.

(SLOPER *puts the bag on the study table and re-enters down* L.,
closing the door behind him.)

SLOPER (*into her face*). Better ! (*He moves to* L. *of the couch.*)

MRS PENNIMAN (*following a step or two*). Well then, you must
see that Morris Townsend would be a feather in any girl's cap.
He's a gentleman. He is handsome, likeable and far and away
the most eligible man that has ever come into Catherine's life.
You should be delighted with this courtship.

SLOPER. Well, before I become too delighted, I should like
to understand it a little better.

MRS PENNIMAN. Let me tell you, Austin, I know a great deal
more about these things than you do. You don't need to understand it. Just be thankful that it has come at all.

(CATHERINE *enters down the stairs.*)

CATHERINE (*in the hall*). I am here, Father.

SLOPER. Yes, Catherine, **my** dear. Come in.

B

CATHERINE (*looking at* MRS PENNIMAN).   Aunt Penniman . . .

MRS PENNIMAN (*moving to* L. *of* CATHERINE).   Would you like to see your father alone, dear ?

CATHERINE (*moving to* R. *of the couch*).   If you wouldn't mind.

MRS PENNIMAN.   Not at all, Catherine.   Not at all.

(*She exits up* C. *to* L.)

SLOPER.   Well, you have something to tell me, Catherine.

CATHERINE.   Yes.

SLOPER.   I shall be very happy to hear it, my dear.   (*He pauses and smiles.*)   Do you suppose that we might both sit down ?

(CATHERINE *sits on the chair* R.   SLOPER *sits on the couch. There is an uneasy pause while he waits, then she blurts out her news.*)

CATHERINE.   I am engaged to be married !

SLOPER.   You do right to tell me.   And whom have you honoured with your choice ?

CATHERINE.   Mr Morris Townsend.

SLOPER.   When was this arrangement made ?

CATHERINE.   Here, this afternoon.

SLOPER.   Before I sat with you both, or after ?

CATHERINE.   Oh, after !

SLOPER.   You have gone fast.

CATHERINE.   Yes, I think we have.

SLOPER.   And you are fond of Mr Townsend ?

CATHERINE.   I like him very much, of course, or I should not have consented to marry him.

SLOPER.   Mr Townsend ought to have waited and told me.

CATHERINE.   He means to tell you tomorrow morning at eleven o'clock.

SLOPER.   It is not quite the same thing, Catherine.   You should not be pleading for him.   He should plead for you.

CATHERINE.   Yes, Father, but I think he is a little afraid of you.

SLOPER.   Is he ?

CATHERINE.   He fears that you do not like him.

SLOPER.   Well, I hardly know him, Catherine, but our liking each other is not important.   The only thing that is important is that he loves you.

CATHERINE.   Yes, Father, that is what he feels.   He so fears to have you think him mercenary.

SLOPER.   Mercenary !   What an odd word for you to use, Catherine.

CATHERINE.   It is not my word, Father, it is his.

SLOPER.   Is it, indeed ?   He doesn't flatter either of us by using it.

CATHERINE. Father, he is a poor man, and I think that has made him sensitive.

SLOPER. Yes, I understand that. But there are many poor men, Catherine, and they don't go through the streets proclaiming that they are not thieves. Especially when no-one has accused them.

CATHERINE. Father, you must try to understand him. He loves me, and I love him. What has happened is very important to me.

SLOPER. It is important to both of us.

CATHERINE (*gently*). Yes, Father, but not equally. My whole happiness is at stake.

SLOPER. I think you exaggerate.

CATHERINE. No, Father, I do not. It is a very great wonder to me that Morris has come into my life. I never expected to meet a man who would understand me as perfectly as he does.

SLOPER. You under-estimate your many qualities, my dear. Well, I have always hoped that some day you'd meet a fine young man who would match your goodness with his own.

CATHERINE (*smiling*). And here I have found the goodness, and with it everything else. Oh, Father, don't you think he is the most beautiful young man you have ever seen ?

SLOPER. He is very good-looking, my dear. Of course, you would not let a consideration like that sway you unduly.

CATHERINE. Of course not ! But that's what is so wonderful to me, that he should have everything, everything that a woman could want—and he wants me.

SLOPER (*decisively*). Well—(*he rises*) I will see him tomorrow.

CATHERINE (*rising ; happily*). I knew you would ! And you are so good that you will be fair and honest with him.

SLOPER (*slowly*). I shall be as fair and honest with him as he is with you.

CATHERINE. Thank you, Father ! (*She kisses him.*) That is all we shall need.

(*She moves up* C. *and exits up the stairs.* SLOPER *stands in thought for a moment then moves into the hall. The church clock strikes the half-hour.* SLOPER *picks up his hat, stick and gloves.* MARIA *enters down* L. *and moves up* C.)

SLOPER (*putting on his hat*). I'm going out, Maria. I must make a call immediately.

MARIA. Oh, but, Doctor, there is a patient waiting for you in your office !

(SLOPER *gives this some thought, then hands his stick and gloves to* MARIA *and moves to the desk.*)

SLOPER. Then you must deliver a note for me.

MARIA (*moving above the couch*). Yes, Doctor.

(SLOPER, *still with hat on his head, sits at the desk and starts to write a note.*)

SLOPER. It is for—(*he writes*) a Mrs Montgomery, who lives in the Second Avenue. (*He continues to write.*) You will have to go to my sister, Mrs Almond, and she will give you the exact address. (*He puts the note in an envelope and rises.*) When you get to Mrs Montgomery's, see that it is delivered directly into her hand. (*He hands the note to* MARIA.)

MARIA. Yes, Doctor. (*She curtsies.*)

SLOPER. You had better take a hack, both ways. Here you are. (*He takes some silver out of his waistcoat pocket and hands her a coin.*)

MARIA. Thank you, Doctor. (*She curtsies, turns to go, then turns back.*)

(SLOPER, *head bowed and deeply preoccupied, starts for his study, crossing below the couch.*)

Your hat, sir. (*She moves* L. *of the couch to him.*)

(SLOPER *turns abstractedly, remembers, removes his hat and hands it to* MARIA.)

SLOPER. Eh? Oh, yes—yes!

He exits down L. *as—*

the CURTAIN *falls.*

SCENE 3

SCENE.—*The same. The following morning.* 10.45 a.m.

When the CURTAIN *rises the room is empty. The chair* R. *of the couch is now back down* R. *The fire is burning cheerfully in the grate. The church clock strikes three-quarters.* SLOPER *enters down* L. *As he does so,* MARIA *enters up* C. *from* L. *She carries a pair of gloves.*

MARIA (*moving down* L.C.). Is anything wrong, Doctor?

SLOPER (L. *of her*). No, Maria.

MARIA. You're home so early from the clinic.

SLOPER. I have an appointment here.

MARIA. Oh! These are Mr Townsend's gloves. He left them here yesterday afternoon. (*She hands the gloves to* SLOPER.)

(*The front-door bell rings.*)

Are you at home, sir?

SLOPER. I am, indeed, Maria!

(MARIA *moves up* L.C.)

If Mr Townsend should call while I am engaged, please show him into my office.

MARIA. Yes, Doctor.

(*She exits up* C. *to* R. SLOPER *puts the gloves on the table* C. *and moves to the fire.*)

(*Off.*) Good morning, Mrs Almond.

MRS ALMOND (*off*). Good morning, Maria.

MARIA (*in the hall*). Dr Sloper is in the front parlour, ma'am.

MRS ALMOND (*in the hall*). This way, Mrs Montgomery.

(MRS ALMOND *and* MRS MONTGOMERY *enter up* C. *from* R. MARIA *closes the front door, then exits up* C. *to* L.)

Good morning, Austin. (*She enters the room and moves above the couch table.*)

SLOPER. 'Morning, Liz.

MRS ALMOND. Mrs Montgomery, this is my brother; Dr Sloper.

(MRS MONTGOMERY *curtsies and shakes hands with* SLOPER.)

Mrs Montgomery has been good to come, Austin. She left a busy household just on the strength of your note.

SLOPER. I am very grateful, ma'am. I should more properly have called on you, but this is one of my mornings at the clinic, and I dared not take the time to make a formal call.

MRS MONTGOMERY. I quite understand, Doctor. I am glad to come. I have occasion to know what the Sloper Clinic has meant for the children of this city.

SLOPER. Have I seen you there, ma'am?

MRS MONTGOMERY. You saw my oldest girl; she had a very bad croup, and you were wonderful.

SLOPER. Well, well, thank you. (*He moves below the couch.*) Mrs Montgomery, will you sit here where we may talk?

MRS ALMOND. Will you excuse me, Mrs Montgomery? I should like to see my sister while I am here.

MRS MONTGOMERY (*sitting on the couch*). Of course, Mrs Almond.

(MRS ALMOND *moves up* C.)

SLOPER. She's in the kitchen, Liz.

MRS ALMOND. Oh, thank you, Austin!

(*She exits up* C. *to* L. *There is a brief pause.*)

SLOPER. It's difficult to begin, isn't it?

MRS MONTGOMERY. No, Doctor . . .

SLOPER (*sitting on the couch, at the* R. *end of it*). You will have gathered from my note that I wish to ask you a few questions.

MRS MONTGOMERY. Yes, I did.

SLOPER. They are about your brother.

MRS MONTGOMERY. Yes, I understood that.

SLOPER. Did you tell him that you were coming here this morning ?

MRS MONTGOMERY. No, Doctor. I thought I would prefer to tell him *after* I had seen you.

SLOPER. Thank you. You must understand my situation, Mrs Montgomery. Your brother wishes to marry my daughter, so I must find out what sort of young man he is. A good way to do so seemed to be to meet you, which I have proceeded to do.

MRS MONTGOMERY (*politely*). I'm very happy to meet *you*, Doctor.

SLOPER. Mrs Montgomery, if your brother marries my girl, her whole happiness will depend on his being a good fellow. I want you to tell me something about his character. What sort of a gentleman is he ?

MRS MONTGOMERY. Well, Doctor, he is intelligent and he is charming. He is a wonderful companion.

SLOPER. Yes, I know that ! But is he reliable ? Is he trustworthy ? Is he—responsible ?

MRS MONTGOMERY. Well, if you mean is he financially secure, he is not, Doctor. But I'm sure you must know that.

SLOPER. Yes, he told me that himself.

MRS MONTGOMERY. That is another thing about Morris. He is honest.

SLOPER (*seizing it*). Is he ? Is he then honest in his feeling for my daughter ?

MRS MONTGOMERY (*gravely*). Oh, I cannot tell you that, Doctor. I never could say what goes on in people's hearts. Could you ?

SLOPER. I have to try, ma'am. As a doctor, I have to try all the time. And now as a father I have to reassure myself that what goes on in your brother's heart will not harm my daughter.

MRS MONTGOMERY. Yes, it is natural to want some assurance. The reason why I came here this morning is that I want that too. I am very anxious that Morris shall make a happy marriage.

SLOPER. Has he always lived with you, ma'am ?

MRS MONTGOMERY. Since he was sixteen, Doctor.

SLOPER. I have only my impression to go by, Mrs Montgomery, but I am in the habit of trusting my impression. Your brother strikes me as selfish.

MRS MONTGOMERY (*calmly*). He is selfish. But then I think we are all rather selfish.

SLOPER. He told me that he had used up a small inheritance. Did he handle it well ?

MRS MONTGOMERY (*smiling*). Probably you would not think so, Doctor, but from his own point of view he did a great deal

with it. He saw Europe, he met many interesting people, he
enlarged his capacities.

SLOPER. Did he help you, ma'am?

MRS MONTGOMERY. No.

SLOPER. Shouldn't he have?

MRS MONTGOMERY. I don't think so.

SLOPER. You are a widow; you have children. *I* think so.

MRS MONTGOMERY. You want me to complain about him, sir.
But I have no complaint. I have brought him up as if he were
my child, and I have accepted the good and the bad in him, just
as I accept them in my children.

SLOPER. I have made you angry, ma'am. I apologize.

MRS MONTGOMERY. I think, Doctor, you expect too much of
people. If you do, you will always be disappointed.

SLOPER. You do not disappoint me, Mrs Montgomery.

MRS MONTGOMERY. And Morris has not disappointed me.

SLOPER (*worriedly*). But you see, these two young people have
only known each other two weeks.

MRS MONTGOMERY (*smiling*). Yes, I know. To me, that is
a good sign.

SLOPER. Is it?

MRS MONTGOMERY. Yes; they are listening only to the
promptings of their own two hearts. They have not taken time
to consider the consequences or weigh the difficulties. They have
just fallen in love.

SLOPER. You mean, at first sight?

MRS MONTGOMERY. Why not? That is the way to fall in
love, if what you see is pleasing.

SLOPER (*looking front*). You know, ma'am, I don't believe in
love at first sight.

MRS MONTGOMERY. It's a matter of temperament, Doctor.
Morris has always made immediate responses to beauty, in any
form.

SLOPER (*looking at her*). In women?

MRS MONTGOMERY (*smiling*). Oh yes, indeed! I hope you
don't think that's a *bad* thing in a young man, Doctor?

SLOPER. No, of course not. (*He rises.*) I want you to meet
my daughter. (*He moves to the staircase and calls.*) Catherine.
Catherine.

(MRS MONTGOMERY *rises, moves to the table above the fireplace and
looks at the miniature.*)

CATHERINE (*off*). Yes, Father?

SLOPER. Will you come downstairs a moment, please?

MRS MONTGOMERY. I am glad I will meet her. I hoped you
would bring us together. (*She picks up the miniature.*) Is this
she?

SLOPER (*moving to R. of her*). No. That is a picture of my wife.

Mrs Montgomery. She is very beautiful.

Sloper. Yes, she was—very beautiful. (*He takes the miniature from her.*)

(Catherine *enters down the stairs and comes into the room.*)

Catherine, this is Mrs Montgomery, Mr Townsend's sister.

(Catherine *is disappointed it is not* Morris.)

Mrs Montgomery. Ah, Miss Sloper. (*She crosses and holds out her hand to* Catherine.)

Catherine (*very shy*). How do you do? (*She curtsies and shakes hands.*)

Mrs Montgomery (*with a curtsy*). I am very happy to meet you.

Catherine. Thank you. (*She indicates the couch.*)

(Mrs Montgomery *sits on the couch, at the* R. *end of it.*)

(*To* Sloper.) Didn't Morris come?

Sloper. No, Catherine.

Catherine (*desperately anxious*). Isn't he coming?

Sloper (*patiently*). His appointment is for eleven, Catherine.

Catherine. Oh, yes! (*She sits* L. *of* Mrs Montgomery *on the couch; with a great effort*). Are your children well?

(Sloper *replaces the miniature on the table above the fireplace.*)

Mrs Montgomery. Quite well, thank you. I hope Morris will bring you to see me and my family very soon.

Catherine (*haltingly*). Yes.

(Mrs Montgomery *and* Catherine *look at each other.* Mrs
    Montgomery *sees that she must start the conversation.*)

Mrs Montgomery. Er—your aunt tells me that you are interested in the hospital charities.

Catherine (*diffidently*). Yes, I am.

Mrs Montgomery. As a doctor's daughter you must be very useful there.

Catherine. I hope so.

(*There is a pause.*)

Mrs Montgomery. My brother tells me that you have an aunt visiting you, Miss Sloper.

Catherine. Yes. Aunt Penniman.

Mrs Montgomery. It is delightful to have people to whom one can show New York. Does she like our city?

Catherine. Yes.

(Mrs Montogomery *goes to speak again, but* Sloper *moves
    down* c. *and speaks.*)

SLOPER. Catherine, perhaps you will offer Mrs Montgomery a glass of the Madeira.

CATHERINE (*rising instantly*). Yes, indeed! Please excuse me. Father, may I ask Mrs Montgomery to try my coriander cookies?

SLOPER (*smiling*). Very well.

(CATHERINE *moves up* C.)

MRS MONTGOMERY. I should like to very much, Miss Sloper.

CATHERINE. I think you will find them quite delicate.

(*She exits up* C. *to* L.)

MRS MONTGOMERY (*after a pause*). She is very shy.

SLOPER. Yes, she is.

MRS MONTGOMERY. Perhaps she is less shy with Morris.

SLOPER. Has your brother listened *only* to the promptings of his heart?

MRS MONTGOMERY. I cannot tell you that, Doctor.

SLOPER. You said, love at first sight. Well, you were right about Catherine. Were you right about your brother?

MRS MONTGOMERY. Well, I—I can only suppose that Morris is more mature in his feelings than I had thought. This time, he has not sought out superficial charms, but has considered the gentle character underneath.

SLOPER. Are you being honest, ma'am?

MRS MONTGOMERY (*looking front*). I think I am.

SLOPER. Well, I think her money is the prime attraction.

MRS MONTGOMERY (*looking at him*). What money?

SLOPER. She is an heiress! Didn't your brother tell you that?

MRS MONTGOMERY. No—he did not.

SLOPER. She has ten thousand dollars a year from her mother, and on my death she will have twice as much more.

MRS MONTGOMERY. She will be immensely rich!

SLOPER. Yes, she will. Of course, if she marries a man I don't approve, I shall leave my part to the clinic.

MRS MONTGOMERY (*rising and moving down* R.; *slowly*). But she has the ten now?

SLOPER. Yes.

MRS MONTGOMERY. That is still a great deal of money, Doctor.

SLOPER. It is. And consider how he has behaved with money. He gratified his every wish. But did he help you with the children? No! He enlarged his capacities in Europe. (*He picks up the gloves.*) He left his gloves here yesterday. (*He moves to* L. *of her.*) Look at them—the finest chamois. Look at yours!

MRS MONTGOMERY (*looking away*). I don't know, Doctor. I don't know.

B*

SLOPER. Will he help you with this fortune he hopes to marry?
I would stake my life that he would not. Yet he has a natural tie
to you—a true affection.

MRS MONTGOMERY (*facing him*). You must follow your own
dictates, Doctor.

SLOPER. Tell me she is not a victim of his avariciousness—
tell me I'm wrong.

MRS MONTGOMERY. I must go now.

(*There is a pause, then* SLOPER *moves* C. MRS MONTGOMERY
moves above the couch.)

SLOPER. Mrs Montgomery, she will believe you. Will you
tell my daughter the truth about your brother's motives?

MRS MONTGOMERY. I don't know the truth, Doctor. I don't
know the truth of anyone's motives.

SLOPER. I think his are clear—pitifully clear. He is in love
with her money. (*He throws the gloves on the table above the couch.*)

MRS MONTGOMERY. You want me to tell her *that*?

SLOPER. Yes.

MRS MONTGOMERY. I won't!

SLOPER. You see, you still protect him.

MRS MONTGOMERY. No, it is the girl I protect. Am I to tell
her that she is undesirable—that she is unloved. Why, it would
break her heart. I would not say that to any girl. (*She moves
into the hall.*)

SLOPER (*moving up* C.). Mrs Montgomery, what am I to do?

MRS MONTGOMERY. I don't know. (*Deliberately.*) But if you
are so opposed to this marriage, then as a father, you must find
a kinder way of stopping it. Good day, Doctor.

(*She curtsies and moves to the front door.*)

SLOPER (*moving into the hall*). Good day, Mrs Montgomery.

(*He moves to the front door and opens it.* MRS MONTGOMERY *exits.*
SLOPER *shuts the door, moves into the room and stands by the
fireplace.* MRS ALMOND *and* MRS PENNIMAN *enter up* C. *from* L.
MRS PENNIMAN *wears outdoor clothes.*)

MRS ALMOND (*moving above the couch*). Oh, was that Mrs
Montgomery leaving? I wanted Lavinia to meet her.

SLOPER. Yes, Liz, she left.

MRS PENNIMAN (*moving* C.). Did you like her, Austin?

SLOPER. Very much.

MRS PENNIMAN. Good! Catherine has just asked Elizabeth
if Marian might be her maid-of-honour.

SLOPER (*turning to the fire*). She must get over it. He is
worthless.

MRS PENNIMAN (*shocked*). What! (*She sits in the armchair.*)

MRS ALMOND. You will not make Catherine see that.

SLOPER (*crossing below the couch to the downstage window*). I will present her with a pair of spectacles.

MRS PENNIMAN (*rising and moving below the couch*). Austin, her entire happiness lies in your hands.

SLOPER (*looking through the window*). That's right, Lavinia.

MRS PENNIMAN. You will kill her if you deny her this marriage.

SLOPER. Nonsense!

MRS PENNIMAN. You will! She is in a pitiable state of anxiety. She passed a dreadful night.

SLOPER (*looking at* MRS PENNIMAN). My dear, people don't die of one dreadful night, or even of a dozen. (*He turns to the window.*) Remember, I'm a physician.

MRS PENNIMAN. Your being one has not prevented you from already losing one member of your family.

SLOPER (*turning angrily*). It may not prevent me, either, from losing the society of another!

MRS PENNIMAN. Oh! (*She sits on the couch.*)

MRS ALMOND. Austin, have you forgotten what it's like to love someone?

SLOPER. I hope not.

MRS ALMOND. Then have some compassion on Catherine.

SLOPER. I can't. She has lacked discrimination; she has been taken in. She must not love people who don't deserve to be loved. I don't. (*He turns to the window.*)

MRS PENNIMAN. Your power to love has withered away.

SLOPER. My judgement hasn't! The man's a fortune hunter.

MRS ALMOND. I don't know, Austin—in these things one can never be sure.

SLOPER (*turning*). Oh, Liz, be sensible! He has walked in here as if this were a shooting box, and Catherine and I were the pigeons.

MRS ALMOND. But you have said yourself she is not a girl likely to attract many men. And if this man likes her, wants to marry her, and will take good care of her, and her money, what is lost?

SLOPER. What assurance have I that he would take good care of her? The contrary is more likely. He has a devoted sister to whom he owes everything, he has never made the smallest attempt to take care of her.

MRS PENNIMAN (*wretchedly*). You have only *her* word for that.

MRS ALMOND (*seeing* CATHERINE *entering*). Ssh! (*She moves a little up* R.)

(CATHERINE *enters up* C. *from* L. *She carries a small silver tray with a decanter of wine, two glasses and a dish of cookies.*)

SLOPER. Mrs Montgomery has left, Catherine.

CATHERINE (*surprised and standing still with the tray*).   Oh, I took too long.   I wanted to make the tray particularly nice.

SLOPER (*moving to* CATHERINE *and taking the tray from her*).   It was not your fault, my dear.   We had concluded our talk.   (*He puts the tray on the table above the couch.*)

(*The church clock starts to strike eleven.*)

CATHERINE.   Concluded ?

SLOPER.   Yes.   (*He moves to the fireplace.*)

CATHERINE.   Did Mrs Montgomery tell you something bad, Father ?

SLOPER.   No, Catherine.

CATHERINE.   I did not impress her favourably, did I ?

SLOPER.   Good heavens, child !   Don't hold yourself so cheaply.

CATHERINE.   I was embarrassed.   I won't be another time.

(*As the last stroke of the church clock is heard, the front-door bell rings.*)

That will be Mr Townsend.

SLOPER.   You had better go to your room, Catherine.

CATHERINE.   Yes.   (*She goes into the hall and turns at the foot of the stairs.   With a great effort.*)   Father—tell him—tell him about me.   You know me so well.   It will not be immodest in you to—to praise me a little.

(*She exits up the stairs.*)

MRS ALMOND (*touched*).   What are you going to do ?

SLOPER.   What *can* I do ?   How is it possible to protect such a willing victim ?

MRS ALMOND.   Austin, you could take her to Europe with you.

MRS PENNIMAN (*rising*).   Oh, no !

SLOPER.   I—I had hopes of going alone.

MRS ALMOND.   I know that.   But this is no time for reliving your memories.   A European trip might be just the thing for Catherine.

(MARIA *enters the hall from* L.)

SLOPER.   See who it is, Maria.

MARIA.   Yes, sir.   (*She moves to the front door.*)

MRS ALMOND.   We will go, Lavinia.

(MRS ALMOND *goes into the hall*.   MRS PENNIMAN *moves up* L.C. MARIA *opens the front door and admits* MORRIS.)

MARIA (*off*).   Good morning, Mr Townsend.

MORRIS (*off*).   Good morning.   Is Dr Sloper at home ?

MARIA (*off*).   Yes, sir.

(MORRIS *enters the hall.* MARIA *puts his hat on the hall table and his stick in the vase, then exits up* C. *to* L.)

MORRIS (*in the hall*). What a pleasant surprise! Good morning, Mrs Almond.

MRS ALMOND. Good morning.

MORRIS. Mrs Penniman . . .

MRS PENNIMAN. Good morning.

MORRIS. Doctor . . .

SLOPER. How do you do, Mr Townsend?

MRS ALMOND. Mrs Penniman and I are just leaving.

MORRIS. Oh, I'm sorry.

(*He enters the room.*)

MRS PENNIMAN. On our way to market. It's such a beautiful morning, we thought . . .

MRS ALMOND (*firmly*). Come, Lavinia, we must be on our way. Good day, Austin. Good-bye, Mr Townsend. (*She goes to the front door.*)

MRS PENNIMAN (*stopping by* MORRIS *on her way to the door*). Mr Townsend, I . . .

SLOPER (*interrupting*). Good day, Lavinia.

MRS PENNIMAN (*to* MORRIS). I—I hope you have a pleasant visit.

MORRIS (*smiling*). Thank you, ma'am. I hope *you* have as pleasant marketing.

SLOPER (*drily*). Good-bye, Lavinia.

(MRS PENNIMAN *is about to speak again.*)

MRS ALMOND. Lavinia!

(MRS PENNIMAN, *flustered, curtsies to* MORRIS, *joins* MRS ALMOND *in the hall and exits with her by the front door.*)

MORRIS (*moving down* C.). You expected me, sir?

SLOPER. Yes, I did. You are admirably prompt.

MORRIS (*smiling*). I deserve no credit for that, Doctor. I could hardly be late for so important an occasion as this one.

SLOPER. Yes. Catherine told me what has been going on between you. Will you sit there? (*He indicates the couch, then closes the sliding doors.*)

MORRIS. Thank you. (*He sits on the couch.*) I have been walking all morning, and you know, sir, I find New York as lovely as any city in Europe at this time of year.

SLOPER (*moving to* R. *of the couch*). Yes. You must allow me to say, Mr Townsend, that it would have been becoming of you to give me notice of your intentions before they had gone so far.

MORRIS. I should have done so, Doctor, if you had not left your daughter so much liberty. She seems to me quite her own mistress.

Sloper.   She **is**.   But she is not, I trust, quite so emancipated as to choose a husband without consulting me.   The truth is, your little affair came to a head faster than I expected.   It was only the other day Catherine made your acquaintance.

Morris.   We have not been slow to arrive at an understanding. My interest in Miss Sloper began the first time I saw her.

Sloper.   Did it not even precede your first meeting ?

Morris.   I certainly had already heard that she was a charming girl.

Sloper (*bringing the chair from* R. *forward*).   A charming girl —that's what you think her ?

Morris (*smiling*).   Otherwise I should not be sitting here.

Sloper (*sitting in the chair*).   My dear young man, you must be very susceptible.   As Catherine's father, I have, I hope, a just appreciation of her many good qualities.   But I don't mind telling you I've never quite thought of her in that light.

Morris (*smiling politely*).   I don't know what I might think of her if I were her father.   I can't put myself in that place.   I speak from my own point of view.

Sloper.   You speak very well—but did you really expect that I would throw my daughter into your arms ?

Morris.   No, I had an idea you didn't like me.

Sloper.   What gave you that idea ?

Morris.   The fact that I'm poor.

Sloper.   That has a harsh sound, but it's about the truth. You have no means, profession, visible resources or prospects, and so you're in a category from which *not* to choose a son-in-law.   Particularly not for my daughter, who is a weak young woman with a large fortune.

Morris.   I don't think Miss Sloper is a weak woman.

Sloper.   Mr Townsend, I've known my daughter all her life —you have known her only two weeks.   Besides, even if she were not weak, you are still penniless.

Morris.   Ah, yes !   *That* is *my* weakness.   And therefore, you mean, I am mercenary.   I only want your daughter's money.

Sloper.   No, I don't say that—*you* say that.   I say simply you are in the wrong category.

Morris (*moving a little* R. *on the couch*).   But your daughter doesn't marry a category.   She marries a man—a man whom she is good enough to say she loves.

Sloper.   A man who offers nothing in return ?

Morris.   Is it possible to offer more than the most tender affection and a lifelong devotion ?

Sloper.   A lifelong devotion is measured *after* the fact. Meanwhile it is usual to give a few material securities.   What are yours ?   A handsome face and figure and a very good manner.

MORRIS. But really, Doctor, I . . .

SLOPER (*rising and crossing to the fire*). Oh, they're excellent as far as they go, but they do not go far enough.

MORRIS (*rising*). There is one thing you should add to them —the word of a gentleman.

SLOPER (*turning; ironically*). The word of a gentleman that you will always love Catherine? You must be a fine gentleman to be sure of that.

MORRIS (*moving to* L. *of the couch*). The word of a gentleman that I am not mercenary. I care no more for your daughter's fortune than for the ashes in that grate.

SLOPER. I take note—I take note. But even with that solemn vow, you are still in the category of which I spoke.

MORRIS. You think I am an idler?

SLOPER. It doesn't matter what I think, once I tell you I just don't think of you as a son-in-law.

MORRIS. You think I'd squander her money.

SLOPER. I plead guilty to *that.*

MORRIS. That's because I spent my own, I suppose. Well, it was just because it was my own that I spent it. And I have made no debts. When it was gone, I stopped. I don't owe a penny in the world.

SLOPER. Allow me to ask, what are you living on now?

MORRIS. The remnants of my property.

SLOPER. Thank you. (*He moves to the table above the couch.*) By the way, you left your gloves here yesterday. (*He picks up the gloves, hands them to* MORRIS *then moves to* R. *of the couch.*)

MORRIS (*taking the gloves*). Thank you. (*He moves below the couch.*) Dr Sloper, don't you care to gratify your daughter? Do you enjoy the idea of making her miserable?

SLOPER (*putting the chair* R. *back against the wall*). I'm resigned to her thinking me a tyrant for a few months.

MORRIS. For a few months!

SLOPER (*turning*). For a lifetime, then. She may as well be miserable that way, as with you.

MORRIS. Ah, you are not polite, sir!

SLOPER (*turning to the downstage window*). You press me to it, you argue too much.

MORRIS (*moving to* L. *of the desk*). Dr Sloper, I have fallen in love with your daughter. I am not the kind of man you would choose for her—and for good reasons. I have committed every folly, every indiscretion a young man can find to commit. I have squandered an inheritance. I have gambled. I have drunk unwisely—I admit. I confess all these things.

SLOPER (*turning and facing him*). Mr Townsend, I am acting in the capacity of a judge, not your confessor.

MORRIS. I tell you these things myself, Doctor, because I love Catherine, and I have a great deal at stake.

SLOPER. Then you have lost it. (*He crosses below* MORRIS *to the doors up* C.)

MORRIS. No, sir.

SLOPER (*opening the* R. *half door*). Just as surely as if you placed your pittance on the losing number. It is over. You have lost.

MORRIS (*crossing and opening the* L. *half door*). Don't be too sure of that, sir. I believe I have only to say the word, and she will walk out of this house and follow me.

SLOPER. You are impertinent!

MORRIS. And may I add, Dr Sloper, if I did not love your daughter as much as I do, I should not have put up with the indignities you have offered me today.

SLOPER. You have only to leave my house to escape them. Good day, Mr Townsend.

MORRIS (*moving into the hall*). Good day, sir.

(MORRIS *picks up his hat and stick.* CATHERINE *enters and calls from the top of the stairs.*)

CATHERINE (*off*). Wait, Morris, wait! (*She runs down the stairs and goes to* R. *of* MORRIS.)

SLOPER. *Catherine!*

CATHERINE. You promised me, Morris, you promised me you would be respectful when you saw my father.

SLOPER (*crossing to the fire*). Catherine!

(CATHERINE *enters the room.* MORRIS *remains in the hall.*)

CATHERINE. What is the matter, Father?

SLOPER. Catherine, you are without dignity.

CATHERINE. I don't care. Why are you angry? Why are you and Morris quarrelling?

SLOPER. Catherine, you must give him up.

CATHERINE. Give him up? Why? What has he done? What did Mrs Montgomery tell you?

MORRIS (*moving to* R. *of* CATHERINE). My sister? Have you spoken with her?

SLOPER. She paid me a visit this morning—on my invitation.

CATHERINE. Father, you must see how painful this is for me; surely you will want me to know your reasons.

SLOPER. He is a selfish idler.

MORRIS. My sister never told you that.

CATHERINE (*holding* MORRIS's *left arm*). But, Father, I know he loves me.

SLOPER. I know he does not.

CATHERINE. In God's name, Father, tell me what makes you so sure.

SLOPER (*after a pause*). My poor child, I can't tell you that— you must simply take my word for it.

CATHERINE. Father, I can't! I can't! I love him! (*Despairing.*) I have promised to marry him, to stay by him, no matter what comes.

SLOPER. So he forearmed himself by getting a promise like that, did he? (*To* MORRIS.) You are beneath contempt!

CATHERINE (*releasing* MORRIS'S *arm; stolidly*). Don't abuse him, Father! (*She pauses.*) I think we shall marry quite soon.

SLOPER. Then it is no further concern of mine.

CATHERINE. I'm sorry.

(SLOPER *moves to the door down* L. *and opens it.*)

MORRIS. Dr Sloper!

(SLOPER *stops and turns.*)

(*With a step forward.*) Dr Sloper, as much as I love Catherine, we cannot marry without your approval. It would bring unhappiness to all of us.

SLOPER. Do you mean that, sir?

MORRIS. Yes.

(SLOPER *closes the door and turns.*)

SLOPER. Mr Townsend, I am going to Europe for six months. I would like Catherine to go with me.

CATHERINE (*moving to* R. *of* MORRIS). *Europe?*

SLOPER. I would like you very much to go, Catherine.

CATHERINE. Why?

MORRIS. Your father thinks you will forget me, Catherine.

CATHERINE. I don't want to go!

SLOPER. Are you afraid? Are you afraid of a separation?

CATHERINE. I shall still love him when I come back.

SLOPER. You are romantic, my dear, and very inexperienced.

CATHERINE. Yes, I am.

SLOPER. And at the moment you are exalted with the feeling of undying devotion to a lover. You are very sure of your love—but, Catherine, do you dare to test him?

CATHERINE (*holding* MORRIS'S *right arm*). You underestimate him.

SLOPER. I do not think so. (*He looks squarely at* MORRIS.)

MORRIS (*after a pause*). Catherine, go to Europe. (*He looks squarely at* SLOPER.) Go to Europe with your father.

CURTAIN

ACT II

Scene i

SCENE.—*The same. An April night, six months later.*

When the CURTAIN *rises* MRS PENNIMAN *and* MORRIS *are seated on the couch with a backgammon board on a stool before them.* MORRIS *is* L. *of* MRS PENNIMAN. *There are empty brandy glasses,* R. *and* L. *of the board. A brandy decanter, half-full, stands on a tray on the table above the couch. The window curtains are closed, the lamps are lit and a cosy glow comes from the fire.* MRS PENNIMAN *shakes the dice and throws them.* MORRIS *leans forward to see the count.*

MRS PENNIMAN. Now this young couple I was telling you about . . .

MORRIS. Well, well, that's just the number you wanted.

MRS PENNIMAN. Why, so it is! (*She moves a checker.*)

MORRIS. Ah, ah, you can't move *that* one.

MRS PENNIMAN. Oh, no, that's right. You have me blocked, haven't you?

MORRIS. Yes.

MRS PENNIMAN. Well, now, let me see. Oh, which one shall I move, Morris?

MORRIS (*smiling and pointing*). That one.

(MRS PENNIMAN *studies the move, then laughs.*)

MRS PENNIMAN. Oh, no, no indeed! I'll do nothing of the sort! That's why you always win!

(MORRIS *laughs, picks up his glass, rises, moves to the table above the couch and puts his glass on it.*)

And this is the night we must settle, isn't it? (*She laughs and takes a note from her bag.*)

MORRIS (*picking up the decanter*). No, no, please. Let your hospitality be full payment. (*He moves to* R. *of her with the brandy decanter.*) May I?

MRS PENNIMAN. No, thank you, Morris. (*She hands him her empty glass.*)

(MORRIS *puts the glass on the table above the couch then holds up the decanter.*)

MORRIS. By the way, what will you say when the doctor asks where his brandy has gone?

46

MRS PENNIMAN. I shall say it was a cold winter and *I* drank it.

(MORRIS *fills his own glass and leaves it on the table.*)

MORRIS. You're right about the cold winter—a lonely one, too. (*Quickly gallant.*) But for your kindness, it would have been unbearable. (*He moves to* L. *of the couch, kisses her hand and sits.*)

MRS PENNIMAN. Oh, thank you, Morris. Now, this young couple I was telling you about. Well, they came to the Rectory long after supper time, and the Reverend Penniman—I miss him so—performed the ceremony without a moment's hesitation. (*With romantic remembrance.*) I was one of the witnesses. The Reverend's assistant, a nice young man, was the other, and do you know, we heard later that the father was reconciled to the young man, and thought the world of him.

MORRIS. And you think the doctor will be reconciled, too ?

MRS PENNIMAN. I'm sure of it. May I see that letter again ?

MORRIS (*taking a letter out of his pocket*). But when I let her go off with him, I thought we would have his consent by now. (*He hands the letter to her.*)

MRS PENNIMAN (*reading*). " February the fourteenth." Almost a month and a half ago. Well, maybe since she wrote that he has given his consent. (*She hands the letter to* MORRIS.)

MORRIS. Maybe. But I cannot take that chance. (*He indicates a place in the letter.*) You see, she says here. (*He reads.*) " I dare not mention your name to Father. He has not been well, and I fear to anger him."

MRS PENNIMAN. You see, she still loves you, Morris.

MORRIS. Oh, yes. (*He puts the letter in his pocket.*)

MRS PENNIMAN. Then you have nothing to worry about.

(*She puts the counters ready for closing the backgammon board.*)

MORRIS (*rising and moving to the table above the couch*). No—if she will really run off with me, I think we can make things come right. (*He picks up his glass.*)

MRS PENNIMAN (*laughing*). I've never kept a secret this long in my entire life.

MORRIS. You must keep it a little while longer, Mrs Penniman. (*He looks at his watch, then at the mantel-clock.*) Good gracious, it's almost nine-thirty. That's the latest we've played all winter.

MRS PENNIMAN (*rising and picking up the backgammon board*). The time passes so quickly. (*She puts the board on the table above the couch.*)

MORRIS (*moving to the fireplace*). It does indeed.

MRS PENNIMAN (*moving* C.). Can I offer you a titbit—a sandwich ?

MORRIS (*sitting in the armchair*). No, thank you. I'm still savouring that excellent dinner.

MRS PENNIMAN. Wouldn't you like to smoke ?

MORRIS. May I ? (*He puts his glass on the table above the fireplace.*)

MRS PENNIMAN. Pray do. (*She moves to L. of the armchair and offers him a cigar from the box off the table above the fireplace.*)

(MORRIS *selects a cigar, takes the band off and tosses it in the fender.*)

MORRIS. Mrs Penniman, you will have to tell Catherine all the details tomorrow. The moment you are alone with her, as soon after the ship docks as possible, you must tell her everything about our plans. And it would be well if she did not unpack. (*He takes a cutter from his pocket and cuts the end of the cigar.*)

(MRS PENNIMAN *replaces the cigar box and picks up the matches.*)

MRS PENNIMAN. Morris, I shall be at the ship at ten o'clock tomorrow morning. (*She strikes a match.*)

MORRIS (*taking the match*). Ten o'clock ? What if the ship docks earlier ? (*He lights his cigar.*)

MRS PENNIMAN. Then I'll be there at seven—at break of day, if it will make you less nervous. (*She puts the matches down and coughs at the cigar smoke as she moves to the stool below the couch.*)

MORRIS. I wish I could have written about this to Catherine.

MRS PENNIMAN (*reassuring*). I shall tell her all the details the moment I see her. (*She brings the stool to R. of the armchair.*)

MORRIS. Yes—but planning an elopement by messenger, it's rather cold.

MRS PENNIMAN (*smiling*). It will be the happiest news she has ever heard. Leave it to me. (*She sits on the stool.*) Morris, I wish I could go with you both tomorrow night.

MORRIS. No, no, you must stay behind to pacify the doctor.

MRS PENNIMAN. Yes, I know—but I would so enjoy it. Think of it ; a private marriage. In the dead of night. Catherine is a lucky girl.

MORRIS (*thoughtfully*). I hope we shall both be lucky.

(*The church clock strikes the half hour.*)

MRS PENNIMAN. Of course you will be. (*She laughs, rises and moves to the couch.*) Austin will be furious.

MORRIS. What ?

MRS PENNIMAN (*sitting on the couch*). Oh, for a few weeks, or a few months, but he will come round.

MORRIS (*unpleasantly reminded*). He told my sister he'd disinherit Catherine. Do you think that's possible ?

MRS PENNIMAN. That was a threat, Morris, and a very foolish one. He can't take away the ten thousand dollars a year Catherine already has.

MORRIS (*musingly*). That would be small comfort.

MRS PENNIMAN (*surprised*). Ten thousand dollars—small ?

MORRIS. On ten, ma'am, you live like your neighbour. Even Arthur and Marian will have ten. But thirty is something to look forward to. On thirty you live—(*his hand takes in the room*) like this.

MRS PENNIMAN. You like this house, don't you, Morris ?

MORRIS (*picking up his glass*). Yes, ma'am, I do. From the first evening I was brought here, I have admired this house, and all the things in it. The doctor is a man of fine taste. It's odd, although we don't like each other, (*he indicates his cigar*) we seem to like the same things.

MRS PENNIMAN. But you are more appreciative than Austin, Morris. Even in the way you have understood Catherine, and responded to her true worth.

MORRIS. Yes, Catherine. (*He handles his wine glass.*) But also other things. For instance, this crystal—it's Venetian. Do you know when I was in Venice, although I was down to my last fifty dollars, I bought two pieces of Venetian glass and kept them for a few weeks just to have them and look at them. Then I was really poor and had to sell them in order to leave. I love such things. I always have. (*He drinks.*)

MRS PENNIMAN. It will be a bond between you when Austin has at last forgiven you.

MORRIS. I hope so. (*He rises and moves* C.) But I'm afraid he'll have contempt for my fine tastes.

MRS PENNIMAN. Why should he, since he shares them ?

(*The sound of a carriage arriving is heard off.*)

MORRIS. He has earned this by his work. He believes that every man should do the same. The trouble is that some of us cannot. (*He puts the glass on the table below the fire.*)

(*The carriage stops.*)

(*He listens.*) What's that outside ? It sounds like a coach. What *is* that outside ?

MRS PENNIMAN. Have we callers ?

MORRIS. You had better look out of the window.

(MRS PENNIMAN *rises, moves to the downstage window and looks out.*)

MRS PENNIMAN (*turning*). Good heavens, they are here.

(*The front-door bell rings, followed by a knock.*)

MORRIS. They are ! (*Trapped, he starts for the hall.*)

MRS PENNIMAN. Morris, don't go ! The brandy ! (*She hastily puts the backgammon board on the table up* R.)

(*Cigar in mouth,* MORRIS *picks up the salver and turns completely round with it.*)

MORRIS. Where shall I put it? (*He puts the salver down again on the table above the couch.*)

MRS PENNIMAN. Oh, go downstairs and wait in the kitchen.

(MORRIS *puts the stopper in the decanter, snatches* MRS PENNIMAN'S *glass from the table and runs into the hall.* MRS PENNIMAN *runs into the hall and calls.*)

Morris ! Your hat ! (*She picks up* MORRIS'S *hat from the hall table.*)

(MORRIS *takes his hat from her.*)

MORRIS. Tell her everything !
MRS PENNIMAN. I will.
MORRIS. Tell her I love her !
MRS PENNIMAN. I will, I will !

(MORRIS *exits up* C. *to* L. MRS PENNIMAN *hurries back into the room and tries to get rid of the cigar smoke by waving her handkerchief.* MARIA *enters down the stairs.*)

MARIA (*running down the stairs*). I think it's them, ma'am.

(*She hurries to the front door and opens it.*)

(*Off.*) Doctor and Miss Catherine, you are really back.

(CATHERINE *enters by the front door. She carries a small dressing-case.* MRS PENNIMAN *moves to the fireplace.*)

CATHERINE (*off*). Yes, Maria, sooner than we thought.

(*She comes into the room.*)

Dear Aunt Lavinia ! (*She moves to* MRS PENNIMAN.)
MRS PENNIMAN. Oh, Catherine ! I am so glad to see you. (*She embraces* CATHERINE.) Why, you are so smart. You look so French, my dear.
CATHERINE. Yes, it's new. Have you been well, Aunt ?
MRS PENNIMAN. Very well !
CATHERINE. Tell me quickly, how is Morris ?
MRS PENNIMAN (*smiling*). The last time I saw him he was very well.

(SLOPER *enters by the front door.*)

SLOPER (*off*). See that those bags go round to the back, Maria.
MRS PENNIMAN. But he told me to tell you . . .
CATHERINE (*with a glance up* C. ; *quickly*). Shhh ! (*She moves below the couch, puts the bag on the* R. *end of it ; her muff on the chair down* R., *then takes her gloves off.*)
MRS PENNIMAN (*moving to* L. *of* SLOPER *in the hall*). Austin, welcome home. But we never expected you.

(MARIA *closes the front door and takes* SLOPER'S *hat and stick.*)

SLOPER. You mean never again, Lavinia? (*He enters the room and moves to the fire.*)

MRS PENNIMAN. I was going to meet you tomorrow with the carriage. (*She moves* C.)

MARIA. I will open the back door for them, sir.

(*She puts the hat on the hall table, the stick in the vase and exits up* C. *to* L. *The carriage departs.*)

CATHERINE. Oh, it is so good to be home! Isn't it, Father?

MRS PENNIMAN. Were you lonely, Cathie?

CATHERINE. Yes, Aunt Lavinia, I was. (*She puts her gloves on the chair down* R. *then takes her fur off and puts it on the chair also.*)

MRS PENNIMAN. Of course you were. No matter how magnificent distant places are, there is always someone at home one misses. Isn't that so . . .?

(SLOPER *moves up* C.)

(*She turns to* SLOPER.) Where are you going, Austin? (*She moves quickly above him.*)

SLOPER. I have a beastly cold, Lavinia. I want some hot water.

MRS PENNIMAN (*moving into the hall*). I'll get it.

SLOPER. I want some brandy too.

MRS PENNIMAN. There's some there—there in the decanter.

SLOPER. Is there? Well! (*He moves to the fire and picks up the brandy glass from the table below it.*) Have you taken to drink, Lavinia?

MRS PENNIMAN. Yes—a little, for my heart. I'll tell Maria about the hot water.

(*She exits up* C. *to* L.)

CATHERINE (*taking off her hat*). I am very glad you decided to leave the ship tonight, Father.

(SLOPER *notices the scent of bay rum and sniffs.*)

You must be as happy to be home as I.

(SLOPER *turns to the fire, and puts the brandy glass on the mantelpiece.*)

(*She moves below the couch.*) I know you have not felt well these last few days, I wish you had let me try to take care of you a little.

(SLOPER *sits in the armchair.*)

Sometimes I almost felt you did not want me by you. (*She puts her hat on the couch and unbuttons her coat.*) It is distressing to be ill away from home. You will be content now that we are back.

(Mrs Penniman *enters up* c. *from* l.)

Mrs Penniman. Maria will be right in. Now tell me everything. I don't care how tired you are. I want to hear everything you did. (*She moves to* Catherine *and helps her off with her coat.*)

Catherine (*smiling*). Dear Aunt Lavinia, that would take a year.

Mrs Penniman. What did you like most?

Catherine. Well, we saw so much.

Mrs Penniman. You loved Paris! Of course you did. It's a woman's city, isn't it. (*She turns to* Sloper.) But you liked it too, didn't you, Austin?

(Catherine *puts her coat and hat on the chair down* r. *then looks at the letters on the table above the couch.*)

Sloper (*rising to* r. *of the armchair*). Is she bringing that hot water?

Mrs Penniman (*moving quickly above* Sloper). Yes, yes, right away.

(Sloper *turns to the fire, notices the cigar band* Morris *has thrown away and picks it up.*)

Well, I don't suppose you want to know what I did all winter. The fact is, I did nothing—nothing at all. (*She sits on the couch.*)

Sloper (*turning with the cigar band on his finger-tip*). Your heart would improve, Lavinia, if you gave up smoking cigars.

Mrs Penniman. What?

(Maria *enters up* c. *from* l. *She carries a small pitcher of hot water and a toddy glass on a tray, which she puts on the stool* r. *of the armchair.*)

Maria. Here you are, Doctor. I can't tell you how glad I am you and Miss Catherine are home, sir.

(Sloper *acknowledges this with a bow, but looks at* Mrs Penniman.)

(*She gets the decanter and puts it on the tray.*) We didn't expect you until tomorrow so the bedrooms are cold. But it will only take a jiffy to lay fires. (*She curtsies.*) They'll be warm in an instant.

(*She turns to* Catherine, *who hands her the clothes from down* r.)

Catherine. Thank you, Maria.

(Maria *curtsies and exits up the stairs.* Catherine *turns to the small mirror on the desk and tidies her hair.*)

Sloper. Well, Lavinia, do you prefer my Massachusetts Home Grown or my Sumatras?

MRS PENNIMAN. I don't know what you are talking about,
Austin.

SLOPER. When I detect the delicious aroma of bay rum—see
my brandy decanter half empty, find loose cigar bands in my
grate, I can only think of one person. Well, what has happened
to Mr Townsend? Has he jumped out of the window?

MRS PENNIMAN. That's right, he did stop by to inquire
about you.

CATHERINE (*moving to* R. *of the couch*). This evening, Aunt?
Has he been here this evening?

MRS PENNIMAN (*embarrassed*). Yes, he just happened to be
in the neighbourhood and stopped by for an instant. (*To*
SLOPER.) I have hardly seen him all winter. He has been most
circumspect.

SLOPER. Really, I should have expected him to make this
house his club. It's a comfortable place to rest in while other
people are working. (*He sits in the armchair and pours hot water
into the toddy glass.*)

MRS PENNIMAN (*nervously*). Catherine, dear, I know I
shouldn't ask, but did you bring me anything?

CATHERINE. Yes, Aunt. A cashmere shawl.

MRS PENNIMAN (*rising*). Just what I asked for! (*She moves
up* C.) Do come and show it to me, dear.

CATHERINE (*moving up* R.). It's in my bag. Maria will unpack
it for you.

MRS PENNIMAN (*moving into the hall*). You will come later,
won't you?

(*She turns to the stairs, sees* CATHERINE *and* SLOPER *are not
looking so exits quietly up* C. *to* L. CATHERINE *moves a little
nearer to* SLOPER, *silently watching as he pours brandy into
his glass.*)

CATHERINE. Father, I hardly expected you would speak that
way of Morris after all this time. Particularly since we have
done everything you asked us to do.

SLOPER. What a ridiculous position to be in. Well, it's a
fitting ending to the most futile six months of my life.

CATHERINE. They were not futile to me. I thought they
were wonderful.

SLOPER. Wonderful! Yes, that's the very word you used,
Catherine. Tintoretto was a wonderful painter; the ices at the
Café Riche were wonderful; almost as wonderful as Michael
Angelo's *David*!

CATHERINE. If you mean I did not appreciate it, you are
wrong. I appreciated everything.

SLOPER. You saw *nothing*, Catherine! What was Rome and
all its glories to you? Just a place where you might receive a
letter from him.

CATHERINE. So that is why you have not let me approach you all these weeks, because I told you I still loved him.

SLOPER. You carried the image of that wastrel with you every place we went. He blotted out any pleasure we might have had. I waited a long time for my trip to Paris. I never thought I should see it all arm in arm with him. Well, there are some things one cannot teach people, even one's own daughter. One cannot give them eyes or understanding if they have none.

CATHERINE. But I have eyes, and I have understanding, Father. You were not thinking of me in Paris—you were with my mother.

SLOPER. I wish I had been! (*He drinks.*)

(*There is a pause.*)

CATHERINE (*moving to the couch*). I see our trip has not changed you. (*She sits.*)

SLOPER. Nor you—nor Townsend. Well, I suppose you'll be going off with him any time now?

CATHERINE. Yes, if he will have me.

SLOPER. Have you! Oh, really Catherine! He ought to be very grateful to me; I've done a mighty fine thing for him in taking you abroad. (*His ironic inflection increases.*) Six months ago you were perhaps a little limited—a little rustic; but now you should be a most entertaining companion.

CATHERINE. I will try to be.

SLOPER. You will have to be very witty indeed, my dear girl. Your gaiety and brilliance will have to make up the difference between the ten thousand dollars a year he'll have and the thirty thousand he expects.

CATHERINE. He doesn't love me for that.

SLOPER. No? What else then, Catherine? Your beauty? Your grace? Your charm? Your quick tongue and subtle wit?

CATHERINE. He admires me.

SLOPER. Catherine, I've been patient with you. I've tried not to be unkind, but now it's time for you to realize the truth. How many women and girls do you think he might have had in this town?

CATHERINE. He finds me—pleasing.

SLOPER. Yes, I'm sure he does. A hundred women are prettier, a thousand more clever, but you have one virtue that outshines them all.

CATHERINE (*fearfully*). What—what is that, Father?

SLOPER. Your money.

CATHERINE (*bowing her head*). Oh, Father. What a monstrous thing to say to me!

SLOPER (*rising with his glass in his hand*). I don't expect you to believe that. I've known you all your life and have yet to see you learn anything. With one exception, my dear—you embroider neatly. (*He moves into the hall.*) Well, since I shan't be at the wedding, I'll drink your health up in my bed. (*He turns.*) Good night, daughter mine !

(*He exits up the stairs.* CATHERINE, *crushed, remains seated, her head bowed.* MRS PENNIMAN *looks in through the door down* L., *makes sure that* SLOPER *has gone, then enters furtively.*)

MRS PENNIMAN (*whispering*). Catherine !

(CATHERINE *turns away.*)

I've got a surprise for you. What would you like most in the world ?

CATHERINE (*without raising her head*). Aunt Penniman, does Morris still love me ?

(MRS PENNIMAN *turns to the door down* L. *and beckons off.* MORRIS *enters quietly down* L. MRS PENNIMAN *exits down* L. *and closes the door softly behind her.* MORRIS *puts his hat on the armchair then moves down* L.C.)

MORRIS. Catherine.

(CATHERINE *hears his voice as in a dream. She looks up and after a moment realizes it is true.*)

CATHERINE. Morris.

MORRIS (*holding out his hands to her*). Yes, it's your Morris, who has waited for you for six months.

CATHERINE (*rising and running to him*). Morris. Oh, Morris ! I'm so pleased to see you.

MORRIS. I couldn't wait another night through. Have you been true to me, Catherine ? Have you been constant, and faithful ?

CATHERINE. Oh yes !

MORRIS. You've not forgotten me ? You've not changed your mind ?

CATHERINE. No, no !

MORRIS. I was afraid you might have. I was full of doubts and fears. That's why I couldn't go home without seeing you. We didn't expect you until tomorrow. I was sitting there when your father knocked on his front door.

CATHERINE (*looking at him adoringly*). You haven't changed, Morris. You are the same as ever. (*She puts her arms around his neck.*)

MORRIS. Has your aunt told you about my plan ?

CATHERINE. Your plan ? (*She breaks from him.*)

MORRIS. For our marriage—our elopement ?

CATHERINE (*bewildered*). Our elopement ?

MORRIS. It is for tomorrow night. At a country parsonage,

up on Murray's Hill : there is a Reverend Lispenard there who knows our story and is prepared to help us.

(CATHERINE *stands transfixed and speechless.*)

Catherine, do you hear me ?

CATHERINE.   Oh, I love you so ! (*She puts her arms around him again, then moves above him and sits in the chair below the fireplace.*)   Tell me what to do.

MORRIS (*kneeling by her*).   I have a closed carriage engaged.   I will come to the corner of the Square at five in the afternoon, before the doctor comes back from his calls.   We will load your trunks, and drive to the parsonage.   After the marriage, we'll spend the night at an inn up the river.   And the next day we'll go on to Albany on our honeymoon.

CATHERINE (*in heaven ; raising his hand to her cheek*).   My husband !

MORRIS.   Do you like my plan ?

CATHERINE.   I think it's wonderful !   I've brought you such a beautiful silk waistcoat.   I'll unpack it and you must wear it for our wedding.

MORRIS.   My dear girl.

CATHERINE.   And I bought you a set of buttons at *Barrere's* in Paris.

MORRIS.   Buttons ?   (*He rises.*)

CATHERINE.   They are rubies and pearls—they are quite nice.

MORRIS (*delighted*).   My dear, dear girl !   (*He kisses her and raises her to her feet.*)   How happy we shall be !

CATHERINE (*disturbed for a moment*).   Morris, my father caught cold on the voyage.   What if he should not go out on his calls tomorrow ?

MORRIS.   Well then, we must wait until the day after.

CATHERINE (*breaking down* L.).   No, I cannot stay here any longer.   (*She turns.*)   I couldn't bear it !

MORRIS.   But it's only one more day.

CATHERINE.   No, Morris, I cannot stay.   (*She moves to* L. *of him.*)   You don't know how it is with me.   (*She has an inspiration and catches hold of him.*)   Morris, take me tonight !

MORRIS.   Tonight !   How can we ?

CATHERINE.   We must !   My cases and bags are all downstairs.   (*She looks at the clock on the mantelpiece.*)

(MORRIS *moves to* C.)

In another hour everyone will be asleep.   We can slip away quietly, no-one will hear us.   (*She moves to him.*)   Morris, I beg you !   I implore you !   If you love me, take me away tonight.

MORRIS.   But where would we go ?

CATHERINE.   To your sister's—or to the Reverend Lispenard.

It won't matter to him that we are one day sooner. And it matters so terribly to me.

MORRIS (*making up his mind*). Very well—we'll do it. (*He looks at the clock on the mantelpiece.*) It's almost ten-thirty. I'll leave and find a carriage. I can be back here with my things packed in two hours. At twelve-thirty on the dot you must be ready, and waiting for me. Can you do that ?

CATHERINE. I can do anything, my dearest !

MORRIS. Now ! We must think carefully of how we shall word your letter.

CATHERINE. What letter ?

MORRIS. The letter you leave for your father. (*He moves to the desk.*) Shall I help you to write it ? (*He sits at the desk.*)

CATHERINE. No.

MORRIS (*taking up a pen*). You must be very clever in it. You must melt his heart. You must make him feel your love and affection.

CATHERINE (*turning away*). I am not going to write to him.

MORRIS (*turning in the chair*). Why, of course, we will write to him. We want him to forgive us.

CATHERINE (*looking at him*). No, Morris, please don't. He won't forgive us, ever. I know that now. I have good reason to.

MORRIS (*rising ; startled*). What reason ?

CATHERINE (*after a pause*). My father (*she looks away*) doesn't like me.

MORRIS (*moving to her*). Why, what an unhappy thing to say. You mustn't think such things. (*He holds her right hand.*)

CATHERINE. It is true.

MORRIS. No, Catherine, your father is disappointed that his plans for you have not turned out as he wanted. He is perhaps hurt, and angry at us both. But that will pass.

CATHERINE (*turning to face him*). No, Morris, it won't pass.

MORRIS. My dear, if I am to be your husband, you must begin to trust my judgement, to rely on me.

CATHERINE. Yes, Morris, I do.

MORRIS. That's right. How often do you think fathers have spoken angrily to the daughters they love, particularly when marriage is the question ?

CATHERINE. He does not love me.

MORRIS. Of course he does ! Indeed he must love you very much, or he wouldn't be trying so hard to protect you. It's only your future happiness he's thinking of.

CATHERINE (*with a step back*). No, Morris. In this one thing I know I am right. I couldn't say it unless I were sure. I understood it tonight for the first time in my life. You can tell when a person speaks to you as if——

MORRIS. As if what ?

CATHERINE. —as if they despised you !

MORRIS. *Despised!*

CATHERINE. Morris, we must be very happy—(*she puts her arms around him*) and you must never despise me.

MORRIS. No, Catherine, of course not.

CATHERINE. We must never ask him for anything. Never expect anything from him. We must be very happy and rely on him for nothing.

MORRIS. No—no.

CATHERINE. I will try to be the best wife in the world.

MORRIS. I know you will. I know you will. (*He is restless.*) Was that a noise? (*He moves up* C.)

CATHERINE (*moving to the fireplace*). Was it my aunt?

MORRIS. I think I'd better go.

CATHERINE (*crossing to the couch and picking up her bag*). I will get ready immediately. (*She moves up* C.)

MORRIS. Yes, you had better. (*He picks up his hat.*)

CATHERINE. I'll try to be punctual, Morris. I know you like that.

MORRIS (*moving into the hall*). Till twelve-thirty, then. (*He moves towards the front door.*)

CATHERINE (*stopping him*). Morris, aren't you going to embrace me?

(MORRIS *turns and takes her in his arms. They embrace.*)

MORRIS. Oh, Catherine! He can't dislike you that much. He's bound to come round.

CATHERINE (*holding him at arm's length*). No, Morris, even if he would, *I* would not.

MORRIS. I see.

(CATHERINE *lifts up her face for a kiss.*)

(*He kisses her.*) Until later, my dear.

He exits quickly by the front door. CATHERINE, *in a state of exaltation, picks up her skirts and runs upstairs as—*

the CURTAIN *falls.*

SCENE 2

SCENE.—*The same. Two hours later.*

When the CURTAIN *rises, the stage is in darkness except for a flicker of light from the fire.* CATHERINE *enters down the stairs. She wears a travelling cloak over her dress. She carries a lighted lamp and her dressing-bag. She puts the bag on the floor* R. *of the hall, puts the lamp on the newel post, then exits up the stairs. After a few moments she re-enters and comes down the stairs. She carries two small bags. She sits on the stool* L. *of the newel post with the bags on her lap. The sound of a carriage is heard. Catherine puts the bags on the floor, rises, moves quickly to the upstage window, opens the curtains and window and peers out. The church clock strikes the half hour. The sound of the carriage fades away into the distance.* CATHERINE *moves into the hall, sits on the stool and puts the bags on her lap.* MRS PENNIMAN *enters and comes down the stairs. She wears a dressing-gown and sleeping cap. She carries a lighted lamp.*

MRS PENNIMAN (*on the stairs*). Catherine !

CATHERINE. Ssh !

MRS PENNIMAN. What are you doing ?

CATHERINE. Aunt Penniman. I would like it if you would please go back to bed.

MRS PENNIMAN (*moving into the hall*). I want to know what you are doing.

CATHERINE. I am eloping with Morris.

MRS PENNIMAN. That's impossible ! It's for tomorrow.

CATHERINE. Ssh ! (*She rises, bags in hand and runs to the upstage window.*)

MRS PENNIMAN (*entering the room and putting the lamp on the table above the couch*). No, no, you have got everything wrong. You have misunderstood him. This is not right, he will be here tomorrow afternoon.

CATHERINE. No, Aunt, he'll be here in the next fifty seconds.

MRS PENNIMAN. Oh ! Why didn't you tell me ?

CATHERINE (*sitting on the stool up* R.). He only slipped away an hour or so ago. I have had to repack all that Maria unpacked. It was hard work. But it was worth it.

MRS PENNIMAN (*scandalized*). Catherine, will you spend the night with him *unwed* ?

CATHERINE. We will drive to the Reverend Lispenard's directly. If he will marry us perhaps we may stay there. If not, we will drive all night. I don't care !

MRS PENNIMAN (*easing* C.). Oh, Catherine, how romantic, how wonderful for you ! Morris is so daring.

CATHERINE (*rising*). Shh ! I think I heard a carriage.

(*They listen for a moment.*)

No.

MRS PENNIMAN (*moving to her*). Catherine, wouldn't you like me to dress quickly and come with you ?

Catherine. No, Aunt, there's no time. Morris will be here any instant.

MRS PENNIMAN. I think I should. If you are to drive all night, you must have a chaperon. Your father would be shocked.

CATHERINE (*moving to the downstage window*). It serves him right. (*She puts the bags on the chair down* R.)

MRS PENNIMAN (*hardly believing her ears*). It serves who right ?

CATHERINE (*opening the curtains and window*). Father—he finds me so dull. It will surprise him to have such a dull girl disgrace his name.

MRS PENNIMAN (*moving to her*). Catherine, are you quite yourself ?

(*There is a sound from the street.*)

CATHERINE (*looking out of the window*). There it is !

(MRS PENNIMAN *looks out too for a moment, then turns back and sits on the couch.*)

MRS PENNIMAN. No, it is a box blowing in the wind.

CATHERINE. To think I may never stand in this window again. That I may never see Washington Square on a windy April night.

MRS PENNIMAN. Why won't you ?

CATHERINE (*turning*). Because I will never be in this house again.

MRS PENNIMAN. Nonsense !

CATHERINE (*gravely*). No, Aunt, it is not nonsense.

MRS PENNIMAN. You will be reconciled with Austin within the year. I guarantee it !

CATHERINE. You had better not do that. (*She moves above the couch to the fire.*) I will never see him again in my life.

MRS PENNIMAN. *What ?*

CATHERINE (*looking at the clock*). What is the time ? Twenty-five to one ?

MRS PENNIMAN. Catherine, come here ! I want you to tell me what you mean.

CATHERINE (*moving to* L. *of the couch ; simply*). I mean, I am leaving tonight instead of tomorrow because it will be one time less that I will ever have to lay eyes on him. Or he on me. We dislike each other too much, Aunt. It is bad for both of us now.

MRS PENNIMAN (*gasping*). But, good God, child, you're disinheriting yourself !

CATHERINE (*serenely*). Yes—completely. (*She moves to the upstage window.*)

MRS PENNIMAN (*rising and moving* L. *of the couch ; horrified*). Have you told Morris this ?

CATHERINE. Of course. I told him everything.

MRS PENNIMAN. Oh, you didn't ! You shouldn't !

CATHERINE. Why shouldn't I ?

MRS PENNIMAN. Oh, Catherine, even if you felt as you did about your father, why did you tell Morris *now* ?

CATHERINE (*moving to the downstage window*). I had to tell him. He is to be my husband.

MRS PENNIMAN. But you should have waited. You should have waited until you were married.

CATHERINE (*looking at her*). We will be married tonight. (*She turns to the window.*)

MRS PENNIMAN. Did he—did he understand ?

(*There is the sound of a carriage in the street.*)

CATHERINE. There he is ! (*Feverishly she gathers up one bag.*) Good-bye, Aunt !

(MRS PENNIMAN *moves quickly to her. They kiss. Then* CATHERINE *runs towards the hall.*)

MRS PENNIMAN (*excited*). Catherine. (*She picks up the second bag, runs to* CATHERINE *and gives it to her.*)

CATHERINE. I will write.

(*She laughs and exits up* C. *to* R. MRS PENNIMAN *goes to the window. The sound of the carriage increases as it nears the house. Then it recedes as the carriage continues on its way. After a pause, we hear the front door close and then* CATHERINE *comes back into the hall.* MRS PENNIMAN *turns from the window.*)

It went by. (*She enters the room and sits on the stool* R. *of the armchair.*)

(*The church clock chimes three-quarters.*)

Aunt Penniman, why shouldn't I have told Morris ? (*She puts one bag on the floor and one in her lap.*)

MRS PENNIMAN (*above the couch*). Oh, dear child, why were you not a little more clever ?

CATHERINE. Clever ? About what ?

MRS PENNIMAN (*moving* C.). About your father's money —about Morris. Oh, Catherine, if you have spoiled this opportunity !

CATHERINE. Spoiled ! In one hour from now Morris and I will be married.

MRS PENNIMAN. I hope so.

CATHERINE. *Hope !* He is only fifteen minutes late. You are ridiculous !

MRS PENNIMAN (*moving below the couch*). No, I am not, Catherine. I know him so well. (*She sits on the couch.*)

CATHERINE (*outraged*). *You* know him ! *I* love him !

MRS PENNIMAN. Morris would not wish to be the cause of your losing your natural inheritance. He could not see you impoverished.

CATHERINE. Impoverished ! We shan't be impoverished. I will have ten thousand dollars a year.

MRS PENNIMAN (*explaining uneasily*). For some people ten would be a great come down. It would be like having none.

C

CATHERINE (*bewildered*). How could it be? It is a great deal of money.

MRS PENNIMAN. Not when one has expected thirty.

CATHERINE. Morris has expected nothing. (*Desperately trying to explain it.*) He loves me! He wants me for his wife.

MRS PENNIMAN. But he would never allow a wife of his to live in an undignified manner.

CATHERINE (*rebelliously*). What is there undignified about it? We shall have more than Marion and Arthur had.

MRS PENNIMAN. Yes, Catherine, but Marian was one of the most popular girls of her year. She was a beauty. She was a belle.

CATHERINE (*after a pause*). You think what my father thinks. You think I am dull and ugly. (*She rises with the bag in her hand and moves to* L. *of the couch.*) Well, you are wrong! Morris loves me! (*As if quoting.*) I am everything he ever yearned for in a woman.

MRS PENNIMAN (*sympathetically*). Oh, Catherine!

CATHERINE. I am! I am! He has told me so. He thinks I am pretty. *He* wants me. He couldn't wait for tomorrow night. He said we must go tonight. (*She remembers the truth with anguish.*) No—I said that, didn't I? I said we must go tonight. (*With sudden hope.*) But he agreed. He was willing. You can see that for yourself. He was very willing.

MRS PENNIMAN (*hopefully*). Perhaps, he will come.

CATHERINE. *Perhaps!* (*She drops the bag.*) Oh, my God! Don't say that to me.

MRS PENNIMAN. What am I to say?

CATHERINE. I can't bear it! I can't bear it another minute. (*Wildly.*) He must come. He must take me away. He must love me!

MRS PENNIMAN. Catherine, you must control yourself.

CATHERINE. No-one can live without that. You can't bear it in the end. (*She sinks to the floor.*) Someone must love me, someone must tell me he wants me, I have never had anyone.

MRS PENNIMAN (*rising and crossing below* CATHERINE *to* L. *of her*). Catherine, dear, you are hysterical.

CATHERINE. Morris is the only one. I have never heard tenderness in anyone's voice but his.

MRS PENNIMAN. I don't think you should say that.

CATHERINE. Why not? Am I not supposed to know it? Am I too dull? That's what my father thinks. He thinks if you are stupid you don't feel. That's not true, Aunt. I'm very stupid, but I've felt everything. (*She kneels up and rests her head on the couch.*) I used to think my misfortune was that my mother died; I don't think that any more. She was so clever, that if she had lived, she too could not have loved me.

MRS PENNIMAN. Catherine, you must take hold of yourself.

CATHERINE (*rising and lying on the couch; weeping*). No, Morris must take hold of me. Morris must love me. Morris must make up for all those who haven't.

MRS PENNIMAN (*moving to her*). Catherine, dear, I have explained it to you. I have told you why he *might* not come.

CATHERINE. You haven't told me how I shall go on living if he doesn't.

MRS PENNIMAN. You have your father (*she kneels beside* CATHERINE) and me, my dear.

CATHERINE (*sitting up*). I have nothing! I have always had nothing. And if Morris has tricked me, then I shall know that no-one has ever loved me in my life. And no-one ever will.

(*As she says this, the church clock strikes one. She listens, and then she breaks down completely.*)

O, my God! My God! (*She bends over racked with pain.*)

MRS PENNIMAN (*softly touching her*). Catherine . . .

CATHERINE. Leave me alone, Aunt. Please leave me alone.

MRS PENNIMAN (*trying to quiet her*). There will be other young men.

CATHERINE (*sitting up*). They would only want what he wants. And I don't want them. I will love him all my life.

MRS PENNIMAN. You will not let yourself be consoled.

CATHERINE (*turning to her*). No, not consoled—(*she turns away again, rocking dully*) loved, Aunt, but not consoled.

CURTAIN

SCENE 3

SCENE.—*The same. Three days later. Morning.*

When the CURTAIN *rises the room is cold with the light of a grey, rainy morning. The front-door bell rings and there is a knock.* MARIA *enters up* C. *from* L., *crosses the hall to the front door and opens it.*

MARIA (*off*). Yes?

MAN'S VOICE (*off*). Is Dr Sloper in, miss?

MARIA (*off*). Yes.

MAN'S VOICE (*off*). Will you ask him to come across the Square to Mrs de Rham's, miss?

MARIA (*off*). Dr Sloper is ill. He isn't making any calls.

MAN'S VOICE (*off*). She's been taken awful bad and we need the doctor right away.

MARIA (*off*). I'm sorry, but Dr Sloper has been laid up for three days himself.

MAN'S VOICE (*off*). What am I to do?

C*

MARIA (off). Try Dr Isaacs in Great Jones Street.
MAN'S VOICE (off). But she wants Dr Sloper, miss.
MARIA (off). I'm very sorry. Good morning.

(*She closes the front door, then stands hesitant at the foot of the stairs. MRS PENNIMAN enters down L. She carries some letters. She is dressed for the street.*)

MRS PENNIMAN. Who was that, Maria?
MARIA (*moving down* C.). It was the de Rham's coachman, ma'am. Mrs de Rham is ill. They want Dr Sloper.
MRS PENNIMAN. Oh, the doctor can't go out.
MARIA. I know, ma'am. I told them to get Dr Isaacs.
MRS PENNIMAN. That was quite right, Maria.
MARIA. Do you think I should tell the doctor about Mrs de Rham? I don't like to disturb him.
MRS PENNIMAN. Oh, he's awake. He's dressing. You have more influence with him than I. You might tell him that it is unwise to come downstairs.
MARIA. Yes, ma'am. (*She curtsies and goes into the hall.*)

(CATHERINE *enters down the stairs.*)

Good morning, miss.
CATHERINE. Good morning, Maria.

(MARIA *exits up the stairs.*)

MRS PENNIMAN (*easing to* R. *of the armchair*). Good morning, Catherine.
CATHERINE (*listlessly*). Good morning, Aunt. (*She sees* MRS PENNIMAN *with the mail and moves quickly to her.*)
MRS PENNIMAN. No, there is nothing, Catherine. They are all for your father.

(CATHERINE *moves to the upstage window and stares out.* MRS PENNIMAN *puts the letters on the table above the couch.*)

(*She watches* CATHERINE *anxiously.*) Catherine, dear, won't you let me get you some breakfast?

(CATHERINE *does not reply.*)

I don't know how long you can go on in this way, Catherine, without food or sleep. I know you were awake most of the night.
CATHERINE. I'm sorry, Aunt, if I disturbed you.
MRS PENNIMAN (*turning away slightly*). You didn't disturb me. I'm just afraid that you are going to be ill.
CATHERINE. Ill?
MRS PENNIMAN (*nervously*). Yes. And with your father ailing. He asked for you again this morning. I do wish you would go in to see him.

CATHERINE (*turning and moving to the table above the couch*). I don't want to see him. (*She looks through the mail.*)

MRS PENNIMAN. Catherine, dear, I told you they are all for your father.

CATHERINE. Yes, I know. (*She moves to the downstage window.*) Aunt Penniman, supposing Morris were ill.

MRS PENNIMAN. Morris!

CATHERINE. Yes.

MRS PENNIMAN. Oh, Catherine!

CATHERINE. Suppose it were something quite sudden.

MRS PENNIMAN. I don't think . . .

CATHERINE (*turning*). If he were ill, he couldn't write, could he?

MRS PENNIMAN. Wouldn't he have sent you some word?

CATHERINE. He is all alone, he has no-one to send.

MRS PENNIMAN. He has his sister.

CATHERINE. But our plan was a great secret. He has not dared confide in her.

MRS PENNIMAN. Catherine, dear, there are many ways of sending you word.

CATHERINE (*with mounting conviction*). That is not true, Aunt. My father is ill and he could not send a message if we refused to take it.

MRS PENNIMAN. Why would his sister refuse him such a thing?

CATHERINE. Mrs Montgomery didn't like me. (*She crosses below the couch to* L.) Morris could well think that I have deserted *him*. That's it! There he lies alone and ill, and for three days I have done nothing.

MRS PENNIMAN (*helplessly*). I can't bear to see you torturing yourself.

(SLOPER *enters down the stairs.* MARIA *is behind him carrying his hat and coat. He is fully dressed and is carrying a small woollen shawl.*)

MARIA (*on the stairs*). But, Doctor, I don't think you should be up at all.

(CATHERINE *turns to the fireplace.* MRS PENNIMAN *moves up* R.)

SLOPER (*on the stairs*). Well, I do. Now stop fluttering about, Maria. I am perfectly well able to walk downstairs. (*He comes into the hall and sees* MRS PENNIMAN *and* CATHERINE.) Good morning, Catherine.

(CATHERINE *does not reply.*)

Lavinia.

MRS PENNIMAN. Good morning, Austin.

CATHERINE (*with her back to* SLOPER). Good morning, Father.

(SLOPER *moves to descend the two steps into the room.* MRS PENNIMAN *moves quickly to* L. *of him to assist.* MARIA *puts the coat on the newel post and the hat on the hall table.* CATHERINE *still faces the fire. Rain is heard.*)

SLOPER. I haven't seen much of you ladies the last few days. Get my things, Maria.

MARIA (*moving to* R. *of him*). But, Doctor, it's starting to rain again. And I'm sure Dr Isaacs will be there right away.

SLOPER. So shall I. Get my bag.

MARIA (*crossing to the door down* L. ; *frustrated*). Oh, Doctor !

SLOPER (*putting on his shawl*). And in the top of that medical box you'll find a black instrument. Bring that with my bag.

MARIA. Yes, Doctor.

(*She exits down* L. *closing the door behind her.*)

MRS PENNIMAN. It's a raw morning, Austin. Better dress warmly.

(MRS PENNIMAN *pulls her shawl around her.* SLOPER *notices the shawl.*)

SLOPER (*moving to the table above the couch*). Are you pleased with your shawl, Lavinia ?

MRS PENNIMAN. Oh, very much, Austin ! You couldn't have brought me a nicer present. (*She moves into the hall and picks up her umbrella and shopping basket.*)

SLOPER (*looking through the letters*). Catherine, did Aunt Elizabeth like her silver tray ?

CATHERINE (*still with her back to him*). I don't know.

SLOPER. But she knows we are back, doesn't she ?

CATHERINE. I don't know.

SLOPER. You mean to say you didn't send her word ?

CATHERINE. No.

SLOPER (*throwing the letters on the table*). But I was ill, Catherine ! You might at least have done that !

(CATHERINE *does not answer.*)

(*He moves into the hall.*) And you, Lavinia, were you too busy to let Elizabeth know we were home ? (*He picks up his overcoat.*)

MRS PENNIMAN (L. *of him*). Catherine wanted a few days to rest. (*An inspiration.*) To get over her seasickness.

SLOPER (*putting on his coat*). Catherine was not seasick.

MRS PENNIMAN. Excuse me, Austin, I must go to market.

(*She moves above* SLOPER *and exits by the front door.* SLOPER *enters the room, buttoning his coat.* CATHERINE *turns from the fire, still with her back to him.*)

SLOPER. Well, Catherine, I have not seen you for three days. You have obviously avoided me. I understand by that that your departure is imminent. It would be a convenience to me to know when I may expect an empty house. When you go, your aunt marches. Is it tomorrow?

CATHERINE. No.

SLOPER. Is it next week?

CATHERINE. No.

SLOPER. The week after?

CATHERINE. I don't know.

SLOPER. Has he asked you to keep your plans secret from me?

(*The rain stops.*)

CATHERINE. No. Will you excuse me, Father? (*She makes an agonized attempt to get out of the room and goes to pass* L. *of him.*)

SLOPER (*stopping her*). Come here a moment, Catherine. Here in the light. (*He leads her by her right wrist, below the couch, taking her pulse as they move. Then,* R. *of her, looks at her closely.*) You are flushed. Have you a little fever?

CATHERINE. No.

SLOPER (*putting his right hand to her temple*). Your eyes look sick. Have you been weeping?

(CATHERINE *drops her head.*)

Oh, Catherine! (*He pauses.*) Have you—have you broken your engagement? If you have, I must tell you, Catherine, I admire you greatly for it. It was a most courageous thing to do. I understand your feelings. I know the effort you must have made.

CATHERINE (*barely audible*). Do you, Father?

SLOPER. I see it's painful still for you to speak of it. I'll not insist. But in time, Catherine, the pain will pass and you will see better how wise and how strong you have been.

(CATHERINE *turns and moves towards the door down* L. MARIA *enters down* L. *She carries the bag and stethoscope. Seeing* CATHERINE *coming, she pauses* L. *of the door.*)

CATHERINE (*almost blindly*). Excuse me, Father, I have some letters to write.

(*She exits down* L. *closing the door behind her.* MARIA *crosses to* SLOPER.)

SLOPER (*taking the stethoscope*). Thank you, Maria.

MARIA (*indicating the stethoscope ; puzzled*). Is that a flute, Doctor?

SLOPER (*taking the bag from her and tucking the stethoscope through the handle*). It's a stethoscope. I got it in Paris. It's for listening to people's hearts. I wish I'd had one long ago. (*He moves into the hall.*) Maria, have something hot for me when I get back, will you?

MARIA (*moving to* L. *of* SLOPER *and handing him his hat and umbrella*). Yes, Doctor, but wouldn't you like me to come with you ? I could carry the umbrella.

SLOPER. No. Stay here with Miss Catherine. Do what you can for her. I'm afraid she's greatly troubled.

MARIA. Yes, Doctor. (*She crosses and opens the front door.*)

(SLOPER *exits by the front door.* MARIA *closes the door after him.* CATHERINE *enters down* L. *She holds a sheet of notepaper.*)

CATHERINE (*calling*). Maria.

(MARIA *enters the room and moves* C.)

Will you do me a favour ?

MARIA (*with a curtsy*). Yes, miss.

CATHERINE. Has my father left ?

MARIA. Yes, miss.

CATHERINE. I have a note here. It's for an address in the Second Avenue. It's very urgent. Will you take it for me ?

MARIA. Yes, miss.

CATHERINE (*relieved*). I will add a line while you get your bonnet.

MARIA. Very well, miss.

(*The front-door bell rings.* CATHERINE *exits hastily down* L., *closing the door behind her.* MARIA *goes into the hall and opens the front door.* MARIAN *enters. She wears a cape and carries an umbrella.*)

(*Off.*) Good morning, Miss Marian.

MARIAN (*off*). Good morning, Maria. (*She moves to the foot of the stairs.*) Is it true that they are back ?

MARIA (*closing the front door*). Yes, ma'am, they got in Sunday night.

MARIAN (*handing her umbrella to* MARIA). So I heard, and I am so provoked about it ! I did want to meet them. Someone should have told us.

(MARIA *puts the umbrella in the vase.*)

MARIA (*taking off* MARIAN'S *cape and hanging it on the newel post*). Well, ma'am, your uncle has not been well, and there was a great deal of unpacking to do. (*She crosses to the door down* L.) I'll tell Miss Catherine you are here. (*She knocks on the door.*) Miss Catherine, Mrs Townsend is here.

(*The door down* L. *is opened quickly and* CATHERINE *stands in the doorway. She still has the note in her hand.*)

CATHERINE. What ?

MARIA. Townsend !

CATHERINE. Townsend ? (*She moves quickly into the room but stops short when she sees it is not* MORRIS.)

MARIAN (*moving to* L. *of the couch*). Yes, I can't get used to being Mrs Townsend either. Welcome home, Cathie. How good it is to see you ! (*She moves to* CATHERINE *and kisses her.*)

CATHERINE. Thank you, Marian.

(MARIAN *and* CATHERINE *move to the couch and sit.* MARIA *closes the door down* L. *and moves up* C.)

Maria, will you be ready to take the note ?

MARIA. Yes, miss, I'll just get my things.

(*She curtsies and exits up* C. *to* L.)

MARIAN (R. *of* CATHERINE; *taking off her gloves*). I should be angry with you, Cathie, but as long as you got home safely I'll forgive you. Did you have a wonderful trip ?

CATHERINE (*slowly*). Yes, it was wonderful.

MARIAN. And to think that Morris Townsend was here to greet you and *we* were not. I'll never get over it.

CATHERINE. Morris ?

MARIAN. Yes.

CATHERINE. Have you seen him ?

MARIAN. Yes, last evening. I was angry with him, too, for not telling us sooner, but he thought we knew.

CATHERINE. What did he say ?

MARIAN. Not much of anything. He just came by to borrow the money for his passage. Arthur didn't want to give it to him. It's an expensive trip to New Orleans.

CATHERINE. New Orleans ? When does he go ?

MARIAN. He sailed last night at midnight.

CATHERINE (*looking away*). So he has gone ?

MARIAN. Yes. And from there he goes to California. He's convinced he'll find gold in California.

CATHERINE (*with the first show of strength*). He will go to great lengths to find it.

MARIAN. I hope he does, for I want him to pay Arthur back. (*Shyly.*) It's costly, having a baby nowadays.

CATHERINE (*looking at* MARIAN). A baby ? Oh, Marian, how pleased you must be.

MARIAN. Oh, yes ! I am ! I am !

(CATHERINE *kisses* MARIAN. MARIA *enters up* C. *from* L. *She wears a cape and carries an umbrella.*)

MARIA (*moving to* L. *of the couch*). I am ready, Miss Catherine.

CATHERINE. Yes, Maria ?

MARIA. For the errand I am to go on. You said it was urgent.

CATHERINE. Oh, that ! It is no longer urgent, Maria. (*She slowly tears up the note.*)

MARIA. Then I'm not to go now, miss?

CATHERINE. No, Maria.

MARIA (*with a curtsy*). Thank you, miss.

(*She exits up* C. *to* L.)

MARIAN. Now tell me about Paris. Where did you buy most of your things?

CATHERINE. At *Madame Talman's*.

MARIAN. How wonderful!

CATHERINE (*with deliberate irony*). She made me everything. Evening clothes, cloaks, and street dresses. And I bought a great deal of every kind of under-linen.

MARIAN (*excitedly*). It sounds wonderful! It's a trousseau for a princess.

CATHERINE. Yes, it is.

MARIAN. And it's so sensible. Any time you decide to marry, you will have everything you need.

CATHERINE. Yes, Marian. There was a shop in Paris where they made only baby things. I bought a great deal there, too.

MARIAN. How sweet of you.

CATHERINE. I bought things in different sizes and both pink and blue trimmings.

MARIAN. That was wonderfully thoughtful. Mother must have written you.

CATHERINE (*after a pause*). I want you to have everything.

MARIAN. Cathie, dear! Of course, there is nothing you could have brought me that I would appreciate more.

CATHERINE. Would you like to see the baby things? I have them unpacked. They are in my room.

MARIAN. Yes, I'd love to!

CATHERINE (*rising*). If you'll come upstairs with me (*she moves to the fire*) I'll show them to you. (*She puts the torn-up note on to the fire.*)

MARIAN (*rising and putting her gloves on the table above the couch*). I'll take very good care of everything. And some day I'll give them all back to you.

CATHERINE (*moving into the hall*). No, Marian, I will never need them. (*She starts to go up the stairs.*)

MARIAN (*moving into the hall*). Why, yes, of course you will.

(SLOPER *enters by the front door.* CATHERINE *is up three or four stairs.*

SLOPER. Marian!

MARIAN. Uncle Austin!

SLOPER. What a cheerful surprise.

(MARIA *enters up* C. *from* L., *above* MARIAN, *and takes* SLOPER'S *hat and stick. She puts the hat on the hall table, the stick in the vase, then exits up* C. *to* L.)

MARIAN. Welcome home. How are you? (*She stands back and looks at him.*) Are you not well?

SLOPER (*taking* MARIAN *by the hand and leading her into the room*). I'm fine, fine. But you—how are you?

MARIAN (*shyly*). Well, I—I am blooming. (*She lowers her head.*)

SLOPER (*patting her shoulder, then putting his bag on the table above the couch*). Oh, good! When are you going to pay me a professional visit?

CATHERINE (*interrupting*). I'll be in my room, Marian.

(*She exits up the stairs.*)

MARIAN. Yes, Catherine. (*To* SLOPER.) When would you like me to?

SLOPER. Come and see me day after tomorrow.

MARIAN. I will.

SLOPER. How is your mother? (*He takes off his overcoat.*)

MARIAN. She is very well, and she will be happy to know that you are home. (*She moves into the hall.*) I must hurry back, Uncle Austin, but first I want to see Cathie's Paris finery.

SLOPER. By all means! And, Marian, come and see her as often as you can, will you? (*He puts his coat and shawl on the stool in the upstage window bay.*)

MARIAN (*on the stairs*). Yes, of course I will.

(*She exits up the stairs.* SLOPER *sits wearily on the couch at the* R. *end of it and closes his eyes.* MARIA *enters quietly up* C. *from* L., *moves into the room and picks up* SLOPER'S *bag.*)

MARIA (*moving to* L. *of the couch*). How was Mrs de Rham?

SLOPER (*opening his eyes with a start*). I don't know. I didn't get that far—I felt quite faint. I lurched against the railing. (*Puzzled.*) I had a little difficulty getting back up our steps.

MARIA. You should have stayed in bed, Doctor. You get up too soon.

SLOPER. Yes, that's probably it.

(MARIA *curtsies and moves down* L.)

Just a moment. I want the—flute.

(MARIA *hands the stethoscope to* SLOPER *then exits down* L. SLOPER, *left alone, proceeds to listen to his chest methodically and carefully just as if he were examining a new patient. He sounds his chest in two places on either side, changing the stethoscope from one ear to the other. As he draws the second breath on his right side,* MARIAN *enters down the stairs, followed by* CATHERINE.)

MARIAN (*moving into the room and picking up her gloves*). Uncle Austin, I'd love to spend a little time and talk to you, but I *must* hurry home. Arthur's mother is coming to lunch.

c**

SLOPER. Yes, yes, I quite understand.

MARIAN (*moving into the hall*). Cathie, dear, I can never thank you enough for those lovely things.

SLOPER (*calling*). Marian! Ask your mother to come by and see me, will you?

(CATHERINE *helps* MARIAN *on with her cape, and hands her the umbrella.*)

MARIAN. Yes, Uncle Austin, I will.

(*She exits by the front door.* CATHERINE *is about to go upstairs when* SLOPER *calls her.*)

SLOPER. Catherine, will you come here a moment, please?

(CATHERINE *moves to* R. *of the couch.* MARIA *enters down* L. *and moves up* C. SLOPER *stops her.*)

Maria.

(MARIA *stops* L. *of the couch.*)

I think you both should know this. I am ill.

(MARIA *takes an involuntary step forward.*)

It's not just a simple congestion—there are already rales in the lungs. I shall need very good nursing. It will make no difference, for I shall never recover——

(MARIA *puts her hands to her face in alarm.*)

—but I wish everything to be done as if I should. I hate an ill-conducted sick-room, and you will be so good as to nurse me on the hypothesis that I shall get well.

(MARIA *looks at* CATHERINE, *who makes no sign.*)

MARIA. Perhaps you will get well.

SLOPER. I am never wrong about these things. Now, in a few days, you will need a doctor for me, get Dr Isaacs. If the street noises make me restless, see that tanbark is put down. And, Catherine, I don't want your Aunt Lavinia in my room at all. Unless I should go into a coma. (*He beckons* MARIA *to come closer.*) As to food, don't overload me, Maria. Keep me on slops. You know, beef broth and gruel.

MARIA. Yes, sir.

SLOPER. Also, hook a large towel round both knobs of my door, so that it doesn't close noisily.

MARIA. Yes, sir.

SLOPER. Find a small lamp; put fresh wicks in it so that it doesn't smell. I want that kept lighted at all times. It's most annoying fumbling round in a dark sick-room.

MARIA. Yes, sir.

SLOPER. Now if you will open up the bed for me, I'll be there in a moment.

MARIA (*on the verge of tears*). Yes, sir.

(MARIA *curtsies, then collects* SLOPER'S *coat and shawl*.)

CATHERINE (*moving up* R.). I will help you, Maria.

SLOPER. Catherine! Catherine! Will you sit with me a minute, please.

(MARIA *exits up the stairs*.)

CATHERINE. If you wish it, Father. (*She sits on the couch,* L. *of* SLOPER.)

SLOPER. You have great emotional discipline, Catherine.

CATHERINE (*not looking at him*). No, Father.

SLOPER. Oh, I admire it. Perhaps we are more alike than I thought.

CATHERINE. Perhaps.

SLOPER. I told you how brave I thought you, my dear. Today, for the first time I see that you have sound judgement, and the courage to carry it through. Seeing that has made my —my present difficulty less important. I can't begin to tell you how proud of you I am, my dear.

CATHERINE. Are you, Father?

SLOPER. Deeply, most deeply proud!

CATHERINE. He jilted me!

SLOPER (*startled*). What?

CATHERINE (*looking at him*). Morris jilted me!

(*The church clock strikes the quarter.*)

SLOPER. Oh, Catherine!

CATHERINE. *Now* do you admire me?

SLOPER (*with compassion*). My poor child! (*He reaches out to* CATHERINE.)

CATHERINE (*turning from him*). Don't be kind, Father! It doesn't become you. He only took *your* estimate of me. You should be elated.

SLOPER. Catherine, I am mortally ill. Don't withhold your natural affection.

CATHERINE. I have no affection for you, Father.

SLOPER (*shocked*). Because I tried to protect you from Morris Townsend?

CATHERINE. No. I see now why you did that.

SLOPER. Ah, then you admit that I was right?

CATHERINE (*looking at him*). No! You thought any clever, handsome man would be as bored with me as you were. And would love me as little as you did. It was not love that made you protect me. It was contempt. Am I to thank you for that?

SLOPER. Some day you will realize I did you a great service.

CATHERINE. I can tell you now what you have done ; you have cheated me. If you could not love me, you should have let someone else try.

SLOPER. Morris Townsend didn't love you, Catherine.

CATHERINE. I know that, now, thanks to you.

SLOPER. Better to know it now than twenty years hence.

CATHERINE. Why ? I lived with *you* for twenty years before I found out that *you* didn't love me. I don't know that Morris would have cheated me or starved me for affection more than you did.

SLOPER. You have found a tongue at last, Catherine. Is it only to say such terrible things to me ?

CATHERINE. Yes, Father. This is a field in which you will not compare me with my mother.

SLOPER (*putting his left hand to his eyes for a moment*). Catherine, Catherine. Should I have let him ruin your life ? I think you are fortunate. You will meet some honest, decent man some day, and make him very happy.

(CATHERINE *rises and moves to* L. *of the couch.*)

You have many fine qualities.

CATHERINE (*turning*). And I will have thirty thousand dollars a year.

SLOPER. Yes. That should make it possible for you to choose with discretion.

CATHERINE. If I am to *buy* a man—I would prefer to buy Morris.

SLOPER (*rising*). Don't say such things !

CATHERINE. Why ? Does it humiliate you ?

(SLOPER *moves to* R. *of* CATHERINE.)

SLOPER. Catherine, promise me—promise me you have done with him.

CATHERINE. No !

SLOPER. Why not ? You know him to be a scoundrel.

CATHERINE. I will not promise.

SLOPER. Then I must alter my Will.

CATHERINE. You should. You should do it immediately.

SLOPER. I will do it when I choose.

CATHERINE (*moving to the desk*). That is very wrong of you. You should do it now while you can. (*She puts the desk chair* R. *of the table above the couch, then brings pen, ink and blotter to the table.*)

SLOPER. I will attend to it tomorrow.

CATHERINE. You may not be well enough tomorrow.

SLOPER (*sitting on the couch, at the* L. *end of it*). I—I spoke hastily. I wish to consider more carefully.

(CATHERINE *dips the pen in the ink, and with the blotter in her left hand, holds them out to him from* R. *of the couch. The blotter has a sheet of notepaper tucked in one corner.*)

CATHERINE.   What is there to consider ?   Since I am unwilling to promise, I should not enjoy your fortune.

SLOPER (*desperately*).   I don't want to disinherit my only child.

CATHERINE.   You want your money used for purposes you approve, don't you ?   *I* certainly should.   If you leave it to the Clinic, it will do what you wish it to do.   If you leave it to me, you know in whose pocket it may end.   (*She almost smiles.*)

SLOPER.   Catherine, I am ill !

CATHERINE (*sitting at the table above the couch*).   You had better tell me how you wish it worded.   (*She prepares to write.*)

SLOPER.   No !

CATHERINE (*writing and speaking the words*).   I, Austin Sloper, Surgeon, of sixteen Washington Square, do hereby make my last Will and . . .

SLOPER (*leaning over the back of the couch and putting his right hand on the blotter*).   Catherine, this is an absurdity !   You can't want me to do it ;   I don't want to do it.

CATHERINE.   I know you don't.   You want to think of me sitting in dignity in this handsome house, rich, respected, and unloved for ever.   That is what you think I deserve.   But I may fool you, Father.   I may take your money and chase after Morris, and squander it all on him.   Which do you think I will do ?

SLOPER.   I don't know.

CATHERINE (*putting the pen down*).   Then, you must decide and act accordingly.

SLOPER (*rising slowly and moving to* R. *of the armchair*).   I can't.   I don't know.

CATHERINE (*rising*).   Perhaps you will in time.

SLOPER (*holding on to the armchair and facing up stage*).   No, I shan't, for I shall be dead.

CATHERINE (*moving up* R. *and facing him*).   That's right, Father, you'll never know, will you ?

SLOPER *sways.* CATHERINE *moves and puts an arm round his waist to help him upstairs as—*

the CURTAIN *falls.*

SCENE 4

SCENE.—*The same.   A summer evening almost two years later.*
     Since SLOPER'S *death,* CATHERINE *has not made much alteration in the room.   The couch and the table above it have gone, and now, an elbow chair stands* R.C., *facing slightly down* R. *The octagonal table stands above the elbow chair, the stool from*

the downstage window bay is now R. *of the elbow chair and a tapestry-frame with an almost completed sampler stands* L. *of the elbow chair. In place of the chair down* R., *there is now a rocking-chair. The stool from the upstage window bay has been removed.*

(See the Ground Plan at the end of the Play.)

When the CURTAIN *rises, it is a warm, summer evening. The windows and curtains are open and the room is lit by lamps on the table up* R. *and the table* C. MRS PENNIMAN *is seated on the desk chair, slightly above the desk. She has an embroidery frame in her lap, and is fanning herself. She is far more coquettishly dressed than she has been previously, although she is still in full mourning. Her lace cap, necklace and bangles make her a rather dressy figure.* MARIA *enters up* C. *from* L. *She carries a tray with a jug of lemonade, two glasses and a bowl of sugar.*

MARIA. Here we are, ma'am. I didn't sugar it. Miss Catherine likes to take her own sugar.

MRS PENNIMAN. Good. Put it there, Maria.

(MARIA puts the tray on the table C. *and mops her face.)*

Is our ice lasting pretty well?

MARIA. I have it wrapped in burlap, ma'am, but I'm afraid it'll be gone by the morning. Even the cellar is hot tonight. *(She opens the door down* L. *for more air.)*

MRS PENNIMAN *(fanning herself)*. Would you and cook like to take a stroll in the Square? Miss Catherine and I will want nothing more.

MARIA. Maybe we will, ma'am. On a night like this, Miss Catherine should be at the seashore.

MRS PENNIMAN. For the last two years she has been saying she prefers the Square to a fashionable beach.

MARIA. She always used to go when Dr Sloper was alive. *(She mops her face again.)*

*(*CATHERINE *enters down the stairs. In her large placid way she is growing into a dignified and almost attractive woman. She is dressed in a filmy, pale dress, a little fussy perhaps, but effective and handsome. She carries some wools.)*

CATHERINE. I have found a whole batch of colours that might do. *(She moves to the desk.)* I hope the moths haven't been at them. *(She gives the wools to* MRS PENNIMAN.)

MARIA *(looking at* CATHERINE; *surprised)*. Why, Miss Catherine, you have changed into one of your Paris gowns.

CATHERINE. Yes, Maria. *(She sits in the chair* C. *and places the tapestry frame before her.)*

MARIA. It is very lovely, miss. And very becoming to you. You look quite handsome.

CATHERINE (*coldly*). It is the coolest dress I could find. (*She commences to sew.*)

MARIA. It's such a hot night, miss, I thought cook and I might take a breath of air in the Square. Do you mind?

CATHERINE. No, Maria.

MARIA (*moving up* C.). Thank you, miss.

CATHERINE. And, Maria——

MARIA. Yes, miss?

CATHERINE. —you are as free in this house as I. When you want a small favour, there is no need to blandish me with false compliments.

MARIA (*surprised*). Miss Catherine! I said what I meant! You *do* look handsome. Doesn't she, Mrs Penniman?

MRS PENNIMAN. Yes, Maria.

CATHERINE (*still sewing*). We will not discuss it. I know how I look.

(MARIA *looks helplessly at* MRS PENNIMAN, *then curtsies.*)

MARIA. Thank you, miss. (*She curtsies to* MRS PENNIMAN.) Good night, ma'am.

(*She exits up* C. *to* L. CATHERINE *stops sewing and sits back with a sigh.*)

CATHERINE. I enjoy my sampler now. It has come on beautifully this summer.

MRS PENNIMAN. Would you not have liked to leave the city for a while, Catherine?

CATHERINE. No, Aunt. (*She sews again.*)

MRS PENNIMAN. But you are young, my dear. Resorts were meant for girls like you. And with your enlarged income you might have taken a lovely house by the sea.

CATHERINE. I prefer it here.

MRS PENNIMAN. It worries me you see so few people.

CATHERINE. I see the people I like.

MRS PENNIMAN. But it is not right! I should *make* you do the things I know are good for you.

CATHERINE (*putting down her needle*). Are you discontented, Aunt?

MRS PENNIMAN. I am content for myself, Catherine, but then *I* am set in my ways. I am getting to be an old lady.

CATHERINE (*rising, and putting the frame downstage of the chair*). Let me give you some lemonade, it will cool you. (*She moves to the table* C. *and pours out one glass of lemonade.*)

(MRS PENNIMAN *puts her embroidery and fan on the desk, rises, glances at* CATHERINE, *then looks out of the downstage window.*)

MRS PENNIMAN (*turning back into the room*). There are so many young couples in the Square. I like to see them.

CATHERINE. If you would like to go for a stroll, Aunt, I will come with you. (*She picks up the fan from the table* C., *moves to* MRS PENNIMAN *and hands her the glass of lemonade.*)

MRS PENNIMAN (*positively*). Oh, no, I don't want to go out!

CATHERINE. Are you tired of your embroidery? (*She sits in the rocking-chair down* R.)

MRS PENNIMAN (*moving above the table* C.). No—er—it hurts my eyes a little. (*She takes a sip of her lemonade, glances at the clock, then puts down her glass on the table* C. *and sits on the stool* R. *of the chair* C.) Catherine, I am going to say something that will surprise you.

CATHERINE (*rocking*). Pray do. I am fond of surprises. And it is so quiet here now.

MRS PENNIMAN (*watching her*). Well, then, I have seen Morris Townsend.

(CATHERINE *stops rocking. There is a dead silence.*)

(*Hurriedly.*) I met him by accident at Marian's. He had only been home a week.

(*The church clock strikes the half hour. There is no sign from* CATHERINE.)

He left there when I did and we walked a little together. He is very handsome, but he looks older and he is not so animated as he used to be. There is a touch of sadness about him—I'm afraid he has not been very successful in California.

(CATHERINE *sits up in her chair and looks towards the window.*)

Catherine, dear, are you listening to me?

CATHERINE. Yes, Aunt.

MRS PENNIMAN (*gathering courage*). He asked ever so many questions about you, Catherine. He heard you hadn't married. He seemed very interested in that. He hasn't married either.

CATHERINE (*rising and moving to the downstage window*). Please say no more.

MRS PENNIMAN. But I must, my dear! He sent you a message and I promised to deliver it. You must let me keep my promise.

CATHERINE (*turning and crossing to the fireplace*). I am not interested in your promises.

MRS PENNIMAN (*rising*). Catherine, he wishes to see you.

(CATHERINE *turns angrily.*)

He believes that you never understood him—never judged him rightly, and the belief has weighed on him terribly.

CATHERINE. How can you bring me such a message? You stood in this room the night he deserted me.

Mrs Penniman.   Catherine, do not say that.   He did not desert you.

(Catherine *sits in the armchair above the fire.*)

(*She moves* c.)   Oh, if you would hear him out—if you would try to understand his side of it.   He meant it nobly, really he did.

Catherine.   I can hear that you have been with him.   He has beguiled you again, and you talk like a fool.

Mrs Penniman.   I don't care what you think of me, Catherine, I am convinced that you will be happier after you have seen him.

Catherine.   You can save your breath, Aunt Penniman.   I will *not* see him !

(*The front-door bell rings.*)

Mrs Penniman (*looking towards the upstage window; distraught*).   Oh, dear !

Catherine.   Who is that ?

Mrs Penniman (*imploring*).   Oh, Catherine . . .

Catherine (*in a stern voice*).   Aunt Penniman, have you dared ?

Mrs Penniman.   Have I done wrong ?   I couldn't help it. I want your happiness so.   It must be right that you see him— you see no-one, Catherine.   Nor does he.   I believe in love like that.   If you are angry at me, don't be.   I am not sensible, I know that, but I want to help.

Catherine.   Aunt Penniman, go to the door, and tell Mr Townsend I am not at home.

Mrs Penniman.   Please . . .

Catherine (*firmly*).   I am not at home.

(Mrs Penniman *goes reluctantly into the hall and opens the front door.*)

Mrs Penniman (*off*).   Good evening, Morris.

Morris (*off*).   Good evening, Mrs Penniman.

(*At the sound of* Morris's *voice,* Catherine *stiffens.*)

It's a long time since I stood here.

Mrs Penniman (*off*).   Yes.   I'm sorry, but Catherine is not at home.

Morris (*off*).   Oh ?   Did you not give her my message ?

Mrs Penniman (*off*).   Yes—but she is not at home.

Morris (*off*).   I see.   (*He pauses.*)   I'm sorry.

Catherine (*calling*).   Come in, Morris.   (*She rises and throws her fan into the chair.*)

(Mrs Penniman *admits* Morris *then exits up* c. *to* l.   Morris *enters the room.*)

Morris.   Good evening, Catherine.

CATHERINE. Good evening.

MORRIS (*moving R. and fanning with his hat*). I have been sitting in the Square for the past half hour watching your windows. I knew you were home. Do I offend you so by coming? (*He mops his face with his handkerchief.*)

CATHERINE. You should not have come.

MORRIS. Didn't Mrs Penniman give you my message?

CATHERINE. I did not understand it.

MORRIS. It's easily understood, Catherine. I have never ceased to think of you.

CATHERINE. Morris, if you cannot be honest with me we shall have nothing further to say to each other.

MORRIS. Very well. I have ventured—I wanted so much to. May we not sit down?

CATHERINE. I think we had better not.

MORRIS. Can we not be friends again?

CATHERINE. We are not enemies.

MORRIS. Ah, I wonder if you know the happiness it gives me to hear you say that.

CATHERINE. Why have you come here to say such things?

MORRIS (*putting his hat on the table up R., then moving C.*). Because since the night I went away it has been the desire of my life that we should be reconciled. I could not break up your life with your father. I could not come between the two of you and rob you of your due.

CATHERINE. My father did not disinherit me, Morris. He threatened it, to test *you*.

MORRIS. But I could not be sure of that, the night I went away.

CATHERINE (*smiling*). No, you could not be sure.

MORRIS. And do you understand what my intention was?

CATHERINE. I have had two years to think about it—and I understand it. So there is nothing further to discuss. I will bid you good night.

MORRIS (*shocked*). But I've come all the way from California to see you—to explain this to you.

CATHERINE. It is late for explanations.

MORRIS (*moving to her; with growing desperation*). Oh, no, Catherine! I would have been back long since—but I have had to beg and borrow the passage money. It has been a real struggle for me to get back here. Why, between New Orleans and Charleston I worked as a hand—a common seaman. Now that I am here you will give me the chance to vindicate myself.

(CATHERINE *studies him.*)

You must hear me out, Catherine. You must!

(CATHERINE'S *expression does not change.*)

Dismiss me later if you like, but hear me out now. For the sake of—for the sake of what we have been to each other, you must hear me out. Please !

(*There is a pause, then* CATHERINE *moves down* C.)

CATHERINE. What is it you wish to explain ?

MORRIS (*above her*). Many things, Catherine, many things. May we not sit down—now ?

CATHERINE. Very well. (*She sits in the chair* C. *with her hands folded in her lap. She does not look at* MORRIS.)

(MORRIS *moves to the desk, brings the desk chair opposite her and sits.*)

MORRIS. Sitting out there I knew just what I wanted to say— but seeing you everything has gone out of my mind. You're changed, Catherine. You've grown into a handsome woman.

CATHERINE. Have I ?

MORRIS. You are so serene.

CATHERINE. I live a quiet life. Perhaps that is why.

MORRIS. How blessèd it must be to live like that, in this lovely house. I've been half across the world since I last sat here, and I tell you, Catherine, you are a lucky woman.

CATHERINE. Do you think so ?

MORRIS. You have everything ; security, position, wealth. No wonder you haven't married ; you had nothing to gain by it.

CATHERINE. No, I had nothing to gain by it.

MORRIS. I have very little to offer you, Catherine, very little except my tenderest affection.

CATHERINE. Sometimes that is a great deal.

MORRIS. Catherine, it was *because* I loved you that I disappeared.

(*She looks at him.*)

I knew that if I returned that night, I might do you a great harm.

CATHERINE. Is this what you have come back to tell me ?

MORRIS. Oh, I know how it looked. It looked as if I behaved abominably, but that was not really the case. I had to be strong for both of us, and I refused to take advantage of your—feeling for me. You know, my dear, no man who really loves a woman could permit her to give up a great inheritance just for him. That is only in the story books. (*He leans towards her imploringly.*) Try to understand me, Catherine. Try not to think of what it looked like, but of what it really was. It was the expression of a husband's love, protecting a wife's future. Can you think of it that way ?

CATHERINE. I will try.   .

MORRIS (*delighted*). You will ! Ah, you're not implacable ! Your aunt feared that you might be.

CATHERINE. My aunt does not know me very well.

MORRIS. Catherine, will you forgive me for the pain I caused you ?

CATHERINE. I forgave you a long time ago.

MORRIS (*rising*). Catherine, dear Catherine, we have only waited, and now we are free.

CATHERINE. How are we free ?

MORRIS. Nothing stands between us.

CATHERINE. You mean you still love me ?

MORRIS. I didn't dare say it.

CATHERINE. Why not ?

MORRIS. I wasn't sure you'd believe me.

CATHERINE. I believed you once, didn't I ?

MORRIS (*sitting on the stool*). It was true then, and it is true now, Catherine. I have never changed. And something tells me you have not, either.

CATHERINE. What tells you that ?

MORRIS. Your expression—your forbearance with me. And the fact that I know you pretty well, and I know how deeply you feel.

CATHERINE. Do you, Morris ?

MORRIS. Perhaps I sound fatuous, but I believe your nature is such that you will always care for me a little.

CATHERINE (*looking away*). Yes, Morris, that is true.

MORRIS (*kneeling ; ardent and hopeful*). Then let us waste no more time, my darling. Let us make the rest of life happy for each other.

CATHERINE. How ?

MORRIS. How ? Why, by picking up where we left off. By doing tomorrow or next week what we were going to do two years ago. By marrying, Catherine !

CATHERINE (*looking at him*). Would you like that ?

MORRIS. Like it ! (*He rises.*) Catherine, you'd make me the proudest and happiest man in the world.

CATHERINE. And what would you make me ?

MORRIS (*sitting on the stool*). Oh, I'd try to be a good husband to you. I am older and wiser now and our marriage would mean a great deal more to me now.

CATHERINE. Why ?

MORRIS. Because I'd know that you loved me and I have come to a place where I need that.˙ I need it more than anything else.

(CATHERINE *rises and moves below the chair to the fireplace, then turns to face him.* MORRIS *rises.*)

CATHERINE. When would you like to marry me, Morris ?

MORRIS. Oh, Catherine ! Then you will ?

CATHERINE. You are as persuasive as ever.

MORRIS (*moving to her*). I mean to be ! Let us marry soon, very soon. After all, we've had our courtship.

CATHERINE. Yes, we have.

MORRIS. Next month?

CATHERINE. You are not as impetuous as you used to be.

MORRIS (*catching hold of her hands*). Impetuous? Why, I would marry you tonight—if I could. (*He pauses.*)

(CATHERINE *looks at him.*)

Would you, Catherine?

CATHERINE (*smiling*). Do you think the Reverend Lispenard is still waiting?

MORRIS (*laughing*). We could tell him we were detained.

(CATHERINE *laughs.*)

Oh, Catherine, would you, really?

CATHERINE. I think I should like that.

MORRIS. Let us do it! Come with me now! We can find a carriage in the Square. Come as you are!

CATHERINE (*breaking from him*). You must give me time to pack.

MORRIS. Yes, of course.

CATHERINE. Where are your things?

MORRIS. At my sister's. We'll pick them up on our way to Murry's Hill.

CATHERINE. Why don't you get them now, and then come back for me?

MORRIS (*taking her by the shoulders*). I will, my dear, I'll run all the way to my sister's, and be back immediately.

CATHERINE (*holding his lapels*). Do you remember the buttons I bought you in Paris?

MORRIS. Oh, yes, the buttons.

CATHERINE. I have them still. Will you wear them tonight?

MORRIS. With great pride and love, my dear. (*He attempts to kiss her.*)

CATHERINE (*avoiding the kiss*). I will get them. (*She moves into the hall and calls.*) Aunt Penniman. Aunt Penniman. (*She turns and looks at* MORRIS.) We could be at Murry's Hill within the hour, could we not?

MORRIS. Yes, by ten.

(CATHERINE *exits up the stairs.* MRS PENNIMAN *enters up* C. *from* L.)

(*To* MRS PENNIMAN.) I am home, really and truly home.

MRS PENNIMAN. What, Morris, what?

MORRIS. She is magnificent.

(MRS PENNIMAN *comes into the room.*)

MRS PENNIMAN. Oh, I am so relieved!

MORRIS (*moving to her*). She is superb. You have done a

wonderful thing for me, Mrs Penniman. (*He kisses her on both cheeks.*)

MRS PENNIMAN. I've never stopped trying, Morris.

MORRIS (*moving to the fire*). She has such dignity now.

MRS PENNIMAN. She's an admirable woman, really she is.

MORRIS. This time I am twice blessed. We are going to be married tonight.

MRS PENNIMAN. Then everything has come true. (*She moves to* MORRIS.) Morris, you will be good to her, won't you?

MORRIS. I will cherish her the rest of my life.

MRS PENNIMAN. And I will see her in a happy home.

MORRIS. Yes. Yes.

MRS PENNIMAN. When is it to be?

MORRIS. We are leaving immediately.

(CATHERINE *enters down the stairs and comes into the room. She carries a small box.* MRS PENNIMAN *moves to her.*)

MRS PENNIMAN. Catherine! Oh, my dear girl! (*She attempts to embrace* CATHERINE.)

CATHERINE (*avoiding the embrace; kindly*). Thank you, Aunt. (*She moves down* C.) Here they are, Morris. Your wedding present. (*She holds out the box to* MORRIS.)

(MRS PENNIMAN *moves down* R.)

MORRIS (*moving to* CATHERINE *and taking the box*). Thank you, my darling. (*He opens the box and looks in.*) Oh, Catherine, they are magnificent! They are rubies. Catherine, they are the most beautiful things I have ever had. Look, Mrs Penniman.

MRS PENNIMAN. Yes, I have seen them. They sparkle so!

(MORRIS *holds one button against his waistcoat.*)

Oh, they suit you, Morris.

CATHERINE. Yes, they do.

MORRIS. I shall cherish them all my life.

(*He attempts to kiss* CATHERINE. *She avoids him by moving below, then to* L. *of him.*)

CATHERINE. Not now, Morris. If we start kissing now we shall never get to the parsonage.

MORRIS. No, no. I'll hurry!

MRS PENNIMAN. How soon will you be back?

MORRIS (*turning to* MRS PENNIMAN; *putting the box in his pocket*). It will be a matter of minutes. Will you turn your head, Aunt Penniman?

MRS PENNIMAN. Oh, yes. (*She smiles and sits in the desk chair.*)

MORRIS (*turning to* CATHERINE). I'll come as soon as I can. We must not waste any more time, my darling.

(*He takes her in his arms and kisses her.* CATHERINE'S *left arm goes up as if to embrace him, but drops again to her side.* MORRIS *releases her and takes her hands.* As he does so, her head goes down.)

(*Earnestly.*) Catherine, you'll have no regrets ?

CATHERINE (*raising her head*). No, Morris.

MORRIS (*kissing both her hands*). For a little while, **then.**

(*He moves up* R., *picks up his hat then exits quickly by the front door.*)

MRS PENNIMAN (*rising*). Oh, Catherine, we have him back !

CATHERINE. Yes.

MRS PENNIMAN. I knew it would turn out this way. *You* were not so sure as I.

CATHERINE. No, Aunt. (*She moves to the upstage window.*)

MRS PENNIMAN (*moving* C.). But I believe in love like this. I hope I always stay romantic. And you know, Catherine, you are much more romantic than you think you are. Morris sensed that.

CATHERINE. Yes, he did. (*She closes the upstage window, and draws the curtains.*)

MRS PENNIMAN. Don't bother about that, dear. I will do it.

CATHERINE. There is no hurry, Aunt.

MRS PENNIMAN. He said he would be right back.

CATHERINE (*moving to the downstage window*). It will take him a little time. (*She closes the window and draws the curtains.*)

MRS PENNIMAN. I've so often read of things like this, and here it has come true in our own lives.

CATHERINE. Yes.

MRS PENNIMAN. That beautiful Paris lingerie—how fortunate that you bought it. *I* am going to pack that for you. (*She moves up* C. *Archly.*) I will sprinkle it with fresh lavender.

CATHERINE. Not yet, Aunt. (*Finished with the window, she goes to her embroidery frame and sits down at it. She picks up her needle.*)

MRS PENNIMAN. But, dear, it's only a stone's throw to his sister's. (*She moves to* R. *of her.*) Oh, dear, you haven't time for *that* !

CATHERINE (*sewing*). I am just working on the "Z".

MRS PENNIMAN. Yes. I know, but don't do it *now.*

CATHERINE. I have only a few more stitches.

MRS PENNIMAN. You will finish it after.

CATHERINE. No, Aunt, I must finish it now, for I shall never do another.

MRS PENNIMAN. That's right ! You have better things to do !

CATHERINE. I have indeed ! I can do anything now !

MRS PENNIMAN (*coaxing*). Come upstairs with me now, dear, you must look your prettiest.

CATHERINE. Sit down, Aunt.

MRS PENNIMAN (*smiling*). Oh, no.

CATHERINE. *Sit down!*

MRS PENNIMAN (*sitting in the chair from the desk*). But, Catherine, Morris will be here . . .

CATHERINE (*sitting up with her hands in her lap*). Morris will have to wait.

MRS PENNIMAN. What!

CATHERINE. He came back with the same lies, the same silly phrases. He thought I was so stupid that I would not detect his falseness. That proves that it is *he* who is stupid, and not *I*. (*She sews.*)

MRS PENNIMAN (*horrified*). No, no, Catherine! That is not true!

CATHERINE. He has grown greedier with the years. The first time he only wanted my money, now he wants my love, too. (*She stops sewing.*) Well, he came to the wrong house, and he came twice. I shall see that he never comes a third time. (*She sews.*)

MRS PENNIMAN (*stricken*). Catherine, do you know what you're doing?

CATHERINE. Yes.

MRS PENNIMAN (*moaning*). Poor Morris.

CATHERINE (*sitting up*). Aunt Penniman, if you ever mention his name again, if you so much as whisper it, I shall understand that you wish to live alone.

MRS PENNIMAN. Catherine!

CATHERINE. I shall take it as a sign that you are leaving Washington Square for ever.

MRS PENNIMAN (*rising ; frightened*). Catherine, can you be so cruel?

CATHERINE. Yes, Aunt, I can be very cruel. I have been taught by masters.

MRS PENNIMAN (*rising and moving to c.*). My dear, life can be very long for a woman alone—I am twice your age, and even I —even I . . .

CATHERINE (*still sewing*). Good night, Aunt.

(MRS PENNIMAN *exits up the stairs.* CATHERINE *concentrates on her sewing. The sound of a carriage is heard approaching.* CATHERINE *listens to it. It stops outside the house. There is a pause, then the front-door bell rings.* CATHERINE, *having finished the sampler, cuts off her cotton and puts the needle and scissors in the work-basket.* MARIA *enters up* C. *from* L.)

(*She calls.*) I will attend to that, Maria. It is for me.

MARIA (*in the hall*). Yes, miss.

(*She curtsies, turns and exits up* C. *to* L. *As she does so, the front-door bell rings again.* CATHERINE *rises and eases the frame a little down stage. The door bell rings a third time, loudly and impatiently.* MARIA *enters up* C. *from* L. *and looks at* CATHERINE.)

(*Puzzled.*) Miss Catherine ?
      CATHERINE (*without looking at* MARIA ; *firmly*). Bolt it, Maria.
      MARIA. Bolt it ?
      CATHERINE. Yes, Maria.

(MARIA *moves to the front door, slides the bolt and puts on the chain. A loud knock is heard on the front door.* MARIA *moves to* L. *of the stairs. There is another knock.*)

(*She moves to the table up* R.) Good night, Maria.
      MARIA (*with a curtsy*). Good night, miss.

(*She exits up* C. *to* L. CATHERINE *extinguishes the lamp on the table up* R., *moves to the table* C., *picks up the lamp from it and goes into the hall. The room is now in darkness. There is a knock on the front door.*)

      MORRIS (*off ; calling*). Catherine. Catherine.

(CATHERINE *looks towards the front door for a few moments, then starts up the stairs. Frantic knocks are heard on the front door.*)

(*Off. He calls.*) Catherine. Catherine.

CATHERINE *exits up the stairs with the lamp, and the light in the hall dims as—*

the CURTAIN *falls.*

FURNITURE AND PROPERTY LIST

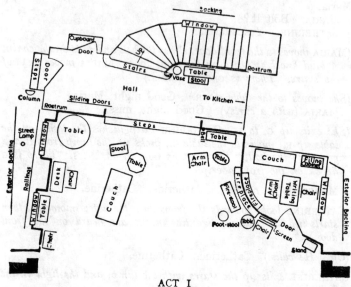

ACT I

SCENE I

On Stage.—Flower stand (*down* L.). *On it :* silver bowl with roses.

Small chair (*down* L.). *Hanging on it :* work-bag with embroidery hoop, with embroidery, threaded needle, thimble, scissors, silks.

Pole-screen.

Sewing table. *On it :* miniature in strong frame.

On mantelpiece : marble and ormulu clock, ornaments, 2 oil-lamps, ashtray, box of matches.

Mirror (*over mantelpiece*).

Fire-basket.

Brass fender.

Fire-irons.

Bellows.

Hearth-brush.

Circular footstool.

Fireside stool.

Wing armchair.

Cabinet table. *On it :* miniature of Mrs Sloper, silver cigar-box with banded cigars.

Oblong table (*up* L.). *On it :* pair of ornaments, vase of roses.

Couch. *On it :* cushions.

88

Pedestal table. *On it :* copy of *New York Times*, silver salver with decanter of sherry and two sherry glasses.

Stool (*above couch*).

Large round table (*up* R.). *On it :* twin oil-lamp, backgammon set, vase of roses, ornaments.

Desk. *On it :* oil-lamp, ink-stand, quill pen, blotter, small mirror, pair of small candlesticks, stationery holder with stationery.

In drawer : birth certificate book, red-covered cardboard cylinder.

Small chair (*at desk*).

Strong coffee-table.

Small chair (*down* R.).

Pair of candle wall-brackets with candles.

China bell-pull.

3 small portraits in oils.

Parquet stage-cloth.

Circular " Aubusson " carpet.

2 rugs.

2 pairs of curtains.

2 pelmets.

Venetian blinds (*not practical*).

Lower sash of each window practical.

In Study.—Writing table. *On it :* oil-lamp, inkstand, blotter, quill pen, a stethoscope of the period, notepaper, envelopes.

Armchair.

Small chair.

Couch. *On it :* folded blanket.

Filing cabinet. *On it :* medical jars.

On mantelpiece : silver cigar-box, miniatures, ornaments.

Brass fender.

Pair of curtains.

Prints and watercolours on wall.

Carpet on floor.

In Hall.—Table. *On it :* oil-lamp, ornaments.

Small stool (*under table*).

Oak bench.

Large oriental vase. *In it :* umbrella

Large oriental vase (*in niche*).

Portraits in oils.

Pair lace curtains.

Pair velvet curtains.

Pelmet.

Stair-carpet.

Carpet runner (*across hall*).

Knocker (*on front door*).

Bolts and chain (*on front door*).

Spring bell (*on front door*).

Windows closed.
Upstage window curtains closed.
Staircase window curtains closed.
Study window curtains closed.
Sliding doors open.
Door down L. open.
Fire on.
Lamps lit.

Off Stage.—Walking-stick, gloves, medical bag (SLOPER).
            Hat and stick (MORRIS).
            Hat and stick (ARTHUR).
            Cape (MRS ALMOND).
            Shawl (MARIAN).

Personal.—CATHERINE : handkerchief.
            SLOPER : watch and chain with spinet key.

SCENE 2

Strike.—Table from c.
         Tray, decanter and glass from table c.
         Glass from mantelpiece.
         Newspaper.
         Sewing-bag.
         All flowers.
         Medical bag from study.
         Cylinder from hall table.
         SLOPER's hat, stick and gloves from hall.
         Clothing from clothes closet.

Set.—Couch down R.C.
       Table above couch.
       Stool in upstage window bay.
       Chair from down R. to R. of couch.
       Barograph on table up L.
       Ornament on stand down L.
       Vase of flowers on table up R.
       Replace lamp from study on desk.
       Desk chair under desk.
       Tidy desk.

Open all window curtains.
Double doors open.
Door down L. closed.
Windows closed.
Fire on.
Lamps out.

Off Stage.—Walking-stick, gloves, medical bag (SLOPER).
            Small packet (CATHERINE).
            Tray. *On it :* decanter of sherry, 2 glasses, dish of biscuits
            (MARIA).

Personal.—MORRIS : watch and chain, sheet of paper with poem.
            SLOPER : coins.

SCENE 3

Strike.—Tray, decanter, glasses, biscuits.
         Small packet.
         SLOPER's hat, stick and gloves.
         Stool from downstage window bay.

Set.—Chair from R. of couch to down R.
       Desk chair under desk.
       Tidy desk.

All window curtains open.
Double doors open.
Door down L. closed.
Windows closed.
Fire on.
Lamps out.

Off Stage.--Pair chamois gloves (MARIA).
      Tray. *On it :* decanter of wine, 2 glasses, dish of cookies
         (CATHERINE).
      Hat and stick (MORRIS).

ACT II

SCENE 1

Strike.—Flowers from table up R.
      Pole-screen.
      Tray, decanter, glasses and cookies.

Set.—Stool below couch.
      Backgammon set on stool.
      2 brandy glasses on stool.
      On table above couch : tray with decanter of brandy (*stopper out*)
      Unopened letters on table up R.
      Matches on table above fireplace.
      MORRIS's hat on hall table.

All window curtains closed.
Double doors open.
Door down L. closed.
Windows closed.
Fire on.
Lamps lit.

Off Stage.—Dressing-case (CATHERINE).
        Tray. *On it :* jug of hot water, glass (MARIA).

Personal.—MRS PENNIMAN : handkerchief, handbag. *In it :* dollar notes.
      MORRIS : letter, cigar cutter.

SCENE 2

Strike.—Letters and salver from table above couch.
      Tray, water-jug and decanter from stool.
      Glass from mantelpiece.
      Lamp from desk.

Set.—Stool from upstage window bay below table up R.
      Desk chair under desk.
      Stool from under hall table to L. of newel post.

All window curtains closed.
Double doors open.
Door down L. closed
Windows closed.
Fire on.
Lamps out.

Off Stage.—Dressing-case (CATHERINE).
      Lamp (CATHERINE).
      2 small bags (CATHERINE).
      Lamp (MRS PENNIMAN).

SCENE 3

Strike.—Stool from R. of armchair.
      2 bags from room.
      Lamp from table above couch.
      Bag from hall.
      SLOPER's hat and stick from hall.
      Lamp from newel post.

Set.—Hall stool under hall table.
  Stool up R. into upstage window bay.
  Shopping basket and umbrella in hall.

All window curtains open.
Double doors open.
Door down L. closed.
Windows closed.
Fire on.
Lamps out.

Off Stage.—Letters (MRS PENNIMAN).
   Shawl (SLOPER).
   SLOPER's hat and coat (MARIA).
   Bag, stethoscope (MARIA).
   Sheet of notepaper (CATHERINE).
   Cape, umbrella (MARIAN).
   Cape, umbrella (MARIA).

SCENE 4

Strike.—Couch.
  Table above couch.
  Chair from down R.
  Stool from upstage window bay.
  Cigar-box and matches from table L. of armchair.
  Backgammon set.
  SLOPER's hat and stick from hall.
  Lamp from hall table.

Set.—Elbow chair R.C.
  Octagonal table above elbow chair. *On it :* lamp, straw fan.
  Stool from downstage window bay to R. of elbow chair.
   On it : work-basket, thimble, scissors.
  Sampler in stand-frame L. of elbow chair.
  Rocking-chair down R.
  Desk chair upstage of desk.
  Ferns in fireplace.
  Vases of flowers as dressing.
  On desk : embroidery frame, fan.

Window curtains open in room.
Window curtains in hall and study closed.
Door down L. closed.
Windows open.
Double doors open.
Fire off.
Lamp on table C. on.
Lamp on table up R. on.

Off Stage.—Tray. *On it :* **glass jug of lemonade, two glasses, bowl of**
     sugar with spoon (MARIA).
   Bundle of wools (CATHERINE).
   Small case of ruby and **pearl buttons** (CATHERINE).

Personal.—MORRIS : handkerchief.

LIGHTING PLOT

Property fittings required :
  Fire in grate, practical.
  4 Table Oil-Lamps, not portable, practical.
  2 Table Oil-Lamps, portable, practical.
  2 Candle Wall-Brackets, not practical.

Interior.   The same scene throughout.
The Main Acting Area is c., L.c., and in the Hall.

ACT I SCENE 1
Evening.

The Apparent Sources of Light are 2 Oil-Lamps on the mantelpiece, Oil-Lamp on the table R., Oil-Lamp on the bureau R., Oil-Lamp in the hall, Oil-Lamp in the study.   The fire is alight.

> *To Open.*   All Oil-Lamps are lit.   The downstage window curtains are open, all other window curtains are closed.
> *Cue* 1.   MORRIS takes the oil-lamp off down L.   (Page 14)
> *Check light covering desk R., bring up light in study L.*

SCENE 2
Afternoon, October.

The Apparent Sources of Light are Windows R., Window over stairs, Window in study.   The fire is alight.   Outside the windows there is brilliant sunshine.

> *No Cues.*

SCENE 3
Morning, October.

The same as Scene 2, but the sunlight outside the windows is not so bright.

> *No Cues.*

ACT II SCENE 1
The same as Act I, Scene 1, but all window curtains closed.

> *No Cues.*

SCENE 2
Night.

> *To Open.*   Stage in darkness, except for glimmer from fire.   All window curtains closed.
> *Cue* 2.   CATHERINE enters down the stairs with a lamp. (Page 58)
> *Bring up lights in hall.*
> *Cue* 3.   MRS PENNIMAN enters down the stairs with a lamp.   (Page 59)
> *Bring up more light in hall.*
> *Cue* 4.   MRS PENNIMAN comes down stage into the room and puts the lamp on the table R.C.   (Page 59)
> *Bring up light to cover c. of room, check lights in hall.*

93

SCENE 3

Morning, April.

The same as Act I, Scene 2, but the daylight outside the windows is grey and cold.

No Cues.

SCENE 4

Evening, Summer.

The Apparent Sources of Light are Oil-Lamp on table R., Oil-Lamp on table C.

To Open. Both Lamps lit. Window curtains in room open. All other window curtains closed.

Cue 5. CATHERINE puts out the lamp on the table R.　(Page 87)
Check lights covering table up R.

Cue 6. CATHERINE picks up the lamp from the table C. and moves up into the hall.　(Page 87)
Check all lights in room, bring up lights in hall.

Cue 7. CATHERINE goes upstairs with lamp.　(Page 87)
Check lights in hall.

MADE AND PRINTED IN GREAT BRITAIN BY
LATIMER TREND & COMPANY LTD PLYMOUTH
MADE IN ENGLAND